Iconic PITTSBURGH

THE CITY'S 30 MOST MEMORABLE PEOPLE, PLACES AND THINGS

D1710977

PAUL KING

THE
History
PRESS

Published by The History Press
Charleston, SC
www.historypress.com

Front cover, top left: photo by author; *top center*: Pittsburgh Steelers; *top right*: Wikimedia Commons; *bottom*: photo by Jeffrey Forse.
Back cover: courtesy of the National Archives; *inset*: Library of Congress.

First published 2020

Manufactured in the United States

ISBN 9781467143592

Library of Congress Control Number: 2019951857

This book is dedicated to Sr. Genevieve McCloskey, a high school English teacher who nearly fifty years ago told me this day would come. I don't believe she thought it would take this long.

CONTENTS

CONTENTS

ACKNOWLEDGEMENTS

Publishing your first book is like winning an award, in that there are so many people to thank. I would like to acknowledge my Pittsburgh friends and relatives, who in person or on Facebook provided me with so many names to include that I probably have enough fodder for two or three more books. Many of them also served as sounding boards as I compiled my research and wrote my chapters. I specifically want to acknowledge Bob and Margie Holder, who provided feedback on many of the chapters; Lynn O'Donnell, who was immensely helpful in assisting me in compiling the list; and her husband, Frank, the best baseball historian I know, who helped set me straight on a couple of things regarding Forbes Field. Also, thanks to Anne Madarasz at the Heinz History Center, who vetted the list and actually is responsible for my adding jazz, Mario Lemieux and Dr. Tom Starzl. Anne also provided insight into several of the icons in her role as chief historian at the history center. Finally, my deepest thanks to my wife, Karen, whose love and support pushed me most when I had trouble believing in myself.

THE LONG ROAD BACK HOME

For the first twenty-nine years of my life, I lived in and around Pittsburgh—most of it spent in Duquesne Heights. For the next twenty-nine years, I lived in and around New York City. Since then, I have called suburban Chicago and, now, Burlington, Vermont, home. So, I have lived longer outside my hometown than I did within its environs. And yet, the spirit of Pittsburgh has never left me.

I had explored so many areas of the city during my time there. In high school, I used to ride my bike or walk from my home on Grandview Avenue all the way to Oakland nearly every Saturday to go to the main branch of the Carnegie Library for research on some class paper or project. My friend Rich Boyle and I used to ride our bikes out to South Park in the summer, passing through Mount Washington, Beltzhoover, Knoxville, Mount Oliver, Carrick, Brentwood, Whitehall and Baldwin. By the time I had graduated from Duquesne University, I had friends in virtually every area of the city and Allegheny County. From concerts at the Syria Mosque and Heinz Hall; to the animals at the Pittsburgh Zoo; to the art, science and history at the Carnegie Museum, I absorbed as much of the city as I possibly could and stored it away in the recesses of my brain. I suppose, subconsciously, I knew I wasn't destined to stay, although leaving Pittsburgh was one of the hardest decisions I've ever made. The move ultimately benefited me as a journalist, but I often wonder what path my life would have taken had I stayed.

I continued to wear my love for the Pirates, Steelers and Penguins proudly. I remember exactly where I was when the Pirates lost that heartbreaking game to the Atlanta Braves in 1992, the "Sid Bream" game that kept the Bucs from the World Series: in a hotel bar in Los Angeles. I kept my friend and Duquesne University classmate Dan Blankowski updated during Game 7 of the 2009 Stanley Cup Finals in Detroit—he working a DJ gig in Atlanta and me watching the game in Staten Island, New York. So passionate was I about Pittsburgh sports that, one year, for our company's annual "Secret Santa," a coworker from a branch office halfway across the United States bought me two Terrible Towels—even though we had never met in person.

I talked up the city every chance I got, and I thrilled at the prospect of meeting fellow "ex-Pitts" in my travels across the country. At organizations and companies of which I was a part, I advocated for the city as a possible site for conferences and other meetings. Moving back has—so far—not been an option for me, but the city has never been out of my thoughts.

So, I guess it was inevitable that I would want to craft a story about my hometown. As a young writer, I dreamed of setting my first novel in Pittsburgh. But after nearly forty years as a journalist, writing profiles of people and places is what I have come to enjoy most. I decided to write a profile of my beloved hometown by identifying the people, places and things that I believe best exemplify Pittsburgh. With the help of some friends, I began to put together a list of the people, places and things that I would want others to know about Pittsburgh. The problem, I quickly discovered, was that there was, and is, so much to cherish about the city. The list grew and grew, as everyone I spoke with had their favorites and we all have slightly different memories, based on our age and exactly where in the area we grew up.

To narrow things down, I set one major ground rule. The items on my final list had to have made a major impact on the city—its history, its growth, its recognition by the outside world or its strength as a community. Ultimately, I settled on a list of thirty—eleven people, ten places and nine things. I did fudge a little bit as I pared down the original list. For example, if the Terrible Towel isn't an icon of this city, then nothing is. But how could I leave off the inimitable Myron Cope? So, in the chapter on the Terrible Towel, I pay homage to Myron as well. Similarly, I combined Point State Park and the Fort Pitt Blockhouse. The USX Building, PPG Plaza and the former Alcoa Building also make up one entry because they represent three building materials for which the city is most famous: steel, glass and aluminum.

No list is perfect, and I don't claim this one to be. Nor is it meant to be definitive, but merely representative of Pittsburgh, because there has to be an end to any list. For that reason, Andrew Carnegie and Mary Schenley are included as representative of Pittsburgh's "Golden Age" because of what they gave back to the city. This isn't meant to diminish the influence of people such as the Mellons and the Fricks.

Inclines are on the list because their appearance and use helped shape Pittsburgh economically and demographically. Streetcars, however, did not make the cut because their role as a mode of transportation was not any greater in Pittsburgh than was their use in scores of other cities around the country. I left off most celebrities, because I didn't want to play favorites. You could take any celebrity category—sports, music, acting—and choose dozens of people for each whose ties to Pittsburgh are noteworthy. If any readers feel strongly about "icons" I left off the list, let me know. Perhaps I'll do *Iconic Pittsburgh II.*

In putting together *Iconic Pittsburgh*, I derived as much pleasure from the research as I did from the writing. I learned scores of things about the city that I had never known and refreshed my memory on many others. In the process, I fell in love with the city all over again. Who knows? I might even return one day for good. But even if I don't, Pittsburgh will always be where my heart lives.

PART I

People

1

ANDREW CARNEGIE

MAN OF STEEL

Pittsburgh was always destined to be a great manufacturing city. It was preordained by the three rivers on which the city was founded and by the vast amounts of coal in its earth. But the ability of a young Andrew Carnegie to understand the value of switching from iron to steel for construction definitely played a pivotal role in what would become Pittsburgh's legacy as the Steel City. Construction of his steel mill in 1872 was the catalyst for not only a steel revolution in the city—at its apex, Pittsburgh had more than three hundred steel-based companies—but also a population explosion. From 1870 to 1910, the city grew from 86,000 citizens to 533,000, making Pittsburgh the eighth-largest city in the country. (Today, it ranks sixty-second, with a population of about 306,000.)

Andrew Carnegie was seen as many things by different segments of the population: insightful businessman, shrewd investor, self-made man, cunning industrialist, ruthless suppressor of employees' rights, generous philanthropist. All were true, at one point or another, in Carnegie's life. His early investments in businesses such as the oil wells found on the William Story farm in Venango County, from which he turned $40,000 into more than $1 million, allowed him to develop iron mills, eventually founding the Keystone Bridge Works in 1864. He continued to invest in other ironworks, using money he earned from the selling of bonds for railroads and bridge companies. Then, when he saw that steel was better than iron for the manufacturing of such items as railroad tracks, pipes and wire, he built a steel mill in nearby Braddock and began to establish an industrial empire.

Even though he never had much formal schooling, the Scottish-born Carnegie knew the value of education and did everything he could to teach himself. He was an avid reader and a keen student of history. He also learned early on the value of networking. Wherever he worked, he cultivated relationships with bosses and colleagues. Then he leveraged those contacts into advancement and investment opportunities. For instance, in 1853, he was hired by Thomas Scott, superintendent of the Pennsylvania Railroad's Western division, to be Scott's secretary. He worked hard, and Scott took a liking to the young man. When Scott was promoted in 1859, he gave Carnegie his old job of superintendent. He also advised Carnegie on some investments and introduced him to other influential people, such as John Edgar Thomson, president of the railroad.

At the outset of the Civil War, when Scott was appointed assistant secretary of war, in charge of transportation, he named his protégé superintendent of the military railroad and telegraph operation. In this role, Carnegie was instrumental in keeping Northern supply lines and communications open during the first year of the war. After the war, Carnegie continued to invest in iron mills and factories. He also traveled to England to sell bonds for various companies. It was there that he saw a new process for making steel, one developed and patented by Sir Henry Bessemer. (Interestingly, the same process had been developed independently in Pittsburgh, by William Kelly, a businessman and scientist. Unfortunately, Kelly was never able to perfect the process because he lacked the financial resources.) The Bessemer process basically injected air into the molten iron ore to burn off the impurities from the iron.

Carnegie brought this process back to Pittsburgh. In 1873, he opened his steel mill in Braddock, and his financial future was secured. In 1883, Carnegie bought the Homestead Steel Works, and by the late 1880s, his company was the largest manufacturer of steel products in the world. Carnegie was ruthless, cutting prices to put competitors out of business and pouring his profits back into the company. His company remained private, and profits fueled his expansion.

His main partner during this period was Henry Clay Frick, whose company Carnegie eventually acquired a majority stake in. Carnegie was the front man, living in New York City to be close to the companies buying his products, and Frick was the on-site manager. It was a solid partnership until 1892, when the famous Homestead Mill strike occurred.

Workers at the mill were members of the Amalgamated Association of Iron and Steel Workers. Carnegie was actually a supporter of unions, arguing

Andrew Carnegie, circa 1896. *Library of Congress.*

that workers had the right to negotiate with management and, if necessary, go on strike to fight for their demands. Carnegie had no problem with this, so long as it was done peacefully. He believed that all disagreements could ultimately be settled without violence.

By 1892, automation at the Homestead Works had eliminated a significant number of jobs. Frick, in his capacity as manager, was negotiating a new contract with workers. He wanted to reduce the minimum wage; he thought he had leverage over the workers because, with fewer jobs, men would rather earn less money than no money at all. The union refused this notion and decided to strike.

At the time of the strike, Carnegie was in Scotland. However, he had telegraphed Frick with instructions that, in the event of a strike, he was to close down the plant. Frick, however, decided that he would try to bust the union by keeping the mill open with "scabs." A gunfight broke out between striking workers and men from the Pinkerton Agency, who had arrived by barge to force strikers away from the gates. Eight men, including five strikers, were killed and dozens more injured.

Although the altercation had been caused by Frick's actions, Carnegie was blamed as well, for his absence and his lack of meaningful action.

By the end of the nineteenth century, Carnegie had decided that it was time to retire and get busy realizing the third part of his "life plan." Early on, he had decided that there were three phases to a successful man's life: first, to get as much education as one could; second, to make as much money as one could, and third, to use that money to help others. Carnegie had already begun to practice that third phase even before 1901, when he decided to sell his company to J.P. Morgan's new United States Steel Corporation. In 1883, he opened the first Carnegie library, in his birthplace of Dunfermline, Scotland. In 1885, he gave the City of Pittsburgh $500,000 for a public library, and the next year, he gave another $250,000 to Allegheny City (now the North Side of Pittsburgh) for a library and a music hall.

But Carnegie was not a man willing to give his money to just any charity; he believed in donating to or establishing those causes that could help young people achieve what he believed their goal should be: education. He was quite able to so do after he sold his company; his share of the sale was $225 million.

Among his most noteworthy philanthropic efforts in Pittsburgh, besides the libraries, were the $2 million he gave to create the Carnegie Institute of Technology (now Carnegie Mellon University) and to construct the Carnegie Institute of Pittsburgh, which features a museum, art gallery and music hall.

His donations to other causes sometimes came back to benefit Pittsburgh in some form. For instance, in 1899, he helped fund an archaeological dig in southeastern Wyoming. Among the finds by paleontologists were the bones of a diplodocus. The bones were brought back to the Carnegie Museum of Natural History in Pittsburgh, and John Bell Hatcher, curator of the museum, named the dinosaur *Diplodocus carnegii* in Andrew Carnegie's honor. Another dinosaur at the museum—*Apatosaurus louisae*—is named after Carnegie's wife, Louise Whitfield Carnegie.

2

HENRY J. HEINZ

KING OF CONDIMENTS

*I*f any native Pittsburgher embodies the work ethic that this city has been known for, it would be Henry John Heinz. Born in 1844, Heinz spent virtually his entire life working—he began his career at the age of nine, when he began selling homemade grated horseradish in downtown Pittsburgh. By the age of twelve, he was gardening on nearly 130,000 square feet of land, selling his produce to local markets. By the time he graduated high school, he was earning the equivalent of, in today's money, some $43,000 a year and had people working for him. He survived bankruptcy to build a company around what might just be the most well-known condiment brand in the world.

Heinz always had a love of horticulture, working first in his mother's garden helping to grow horseradish. He had a knack for it, leading his parents to give him his own plot for gardening when he was ten years old. Heinz was raised Lutheran, and his mother, Anna, wanted him to become a minister. But young Heinz had caught the business bug, and when he graduated high school, he used the money he had earned as a vegetable seller to finance his education at Duff's Mercantile College.

But he didn't return to the vegetable business right after college. Instead, he went to work at his father's brickmaking business. His education, paired with his innate curiosity, made him a valuable employee. Not only did he make changes to the way bricks were made, in order to improve their quality and speed of production, he also made the business financially sound.

The H.J. Heinz factories, circa 1915. *Library of Congress.*

But he longed to run his own business, so in 1869, he partnered with Clarence Noble and began selling packaged horseradish. Heinz and Noble became wildly successful, primarily because Heinz did something few of his competitors did: he sold his horseradish in clear jars. In doing so, he demonstrated the high quality of his company's product at a time when most companies hid their products inside opaque jars.

Heinz and Noble built up such a reputation that it seemed nothing could stop them, and they began adding more items to their product list. But horseradish remained the number one seller until 1875, when an unusual calamity struck: a banner crop of horseradish in the United States. With an overabundance, the price of horseradish fell precipitously; suddenly, price became more important than quality to customers. Heinz's sales plummeted, and the young man was forced to declare bankruptcy.

Heinz was undeterred, but his financial situation prevented him from forming a new company. So, the following year, he used his brother John and a cousin, Frederick, to create F. & J. Heinz. Henry Heinz worked behind the scenes as the plant manager, and the first product he decided to sell was tomato ketchup.

Ketchup was not an unusual product back then; by 1915, more than eight hundred different brands existed. High-quality ketchup was another story. According to a 2013 article in *Fast Company*, an examination of commercial ketchups in 1896 revealed that more than 90 percent contained "injurious ingredients."

At the time, Heinz was actually one of those brands. Even though Heinz packed its product in clear bottles, and its entire production process was transparent—so proud was Henry Heinz of his company's factories that thousands of people were allowed to tour them each year—a preservative-free ketchup wasn't created until 1904. (Heinz's chief food scientist, G.F. Mason, came up with the process.) Still, Heinz operated perhaps the cleanest, safest facilities in the world, and when the federal government proposed the Pure Food and Drug Act in 1906, Heinz was a huge supporter of the measure.

Not only was Heinz a conscientious manufacturer, but he also was a natural marketer. He found a number of ways to "sell" the Heinz brand. For example, at the Chicago World's Fair in 1893, Heinz figured out a way to draw people to his company's booth, which was located in an out-of-the-way location on the third floor of the Exposition Hall. He had a novelty store make up "pickle pins." Then he distributed cards throughout the hall that entitled the bearers to a "free gift." So many people visited the Heinz booth that, according to some published reports, organizers feared the floor might collapse.

Even the slogan "57 Varieties," which appears on Heinz products, was pure marketing genius. Throughout its history, Heinz has sold any number of products—today, the total is north of six hundred—but it's a safe bet that it never sold just fifty-seven. However, in 1896, when Henry Heinz saw a shoe store that advertised that it sold twenty-one types of shoes, he decided that he needed something similar to promote his company. Smart enough to know that his product list was fluid, he figured the number wouldn't matter. He chose 57.

Several explanations surrounding the selection of this particular number have been offered over the years. One commonly told legend is that the *5* was Heinz's favorite number and *7* was his wife, Sarah's. Other anecdotes ascribe mysticism or some other "magic" to the choice. How it came about doesn't matter. The number worked. So did Henry Heinz's propensity to advertise his name and his company's products anywhere he could. By the early 1900s, Heinz was a celebrity.

Heinz was also a globalist, at least in terms of sales and marketing. When the company sold its first product overseas in 1886, Heinz said, "Our field is the world," and the company has lived up to that claim. His attempts to sell products to far-flung nations also led to what may well be another first that has become commonplace: in-store demonstrations. In Australia, Heinz salesman Alexander MacWillie decided he needed a way to introduce some products, such as relish or baked beans, to customers who had never seen them. So, he hired a woman, Margaret McLeod, to offer free samples and talk up the products in supermarkets. The gimmick not only proved valuable for increasing sales, it also attracted more media attention and enhanced the company's marketing efforts. Today, Heinz is ubiquitous, its products sold in more than two hundred countries and its ketchup accounting for some 60 percent of total ketchup sales worldwide. More important, Henry Heinz's sons and grandsons have maintained his core values: quality, transparency, respect and integrity.

3

DAVID L. LAWRENCE

RENAISSANCE MAN

*T*here is a lot to admire about David Leo Lawrence, a four-term mayor of Pittsburgh and the primary architect of the city's first great renaissance, in the late 1940s and early 1950s. Lawrence is the only Pittsburgh mayor to also serve as Pennsylvania's governor. He rose above what he considered to be anti-Catholic bias in politics to help usher in an era of Democratic dominance in the city. He kicked off an urban renewal that reverberates throughout the city to this day—for reasons both good and bad.

"It's hard to argue that there is another politician who has had a bigger imprint on the city," said Anne Madarasz, chief historian at the Heinz History Center in Pittsburgh. "He was prescient enough to build the coalition that led to the renaissance. He and Richard King Mellon and the Allegheny Conference [on Community Development] had that kind of public-private partnership that was unusual for the times. With regard to urban renewal, whether you agree with the decisions that were made in the late 1940s and into the '50s, people came here from around the world to study what was going on here, and he was at the center of that."

David Lawrence spent an unprecedented thirteen years as Pittsburgh's mayor, his fourth term cut short only because he was elected governor of Pennsylvania in 1958—the state's first Catholic governor. He wielded strong influence on the Democratic Party in Pittsburgh, in the state and even nationally, and he also served Presidents John Kennedy and Lyndon Johnson as chair of the President's Committee on Equal Opportunities in Housing.

Lawrence has been called everything from a "benevolent crook" to a "maker of presidents." His legacy is really somewhere in the middle of those two extremes—except where Pittsburgh is concerned. Because, for all his faults, Lawrence presided over a cleanup that some people despaired could ever be accomplished.

When Lawrence was elected mayor in 1945, Pittsburgh was a hot mess—almost literally. The city's best asset, its manufacturing industries, was also its biggest detriment. Air pollution was at unprecedented levels, and the city's waterways were nearly as bad. "Midnight at noon" was a way of life in Pittsburgh, with the smog so thick that streetlights burned both night and day. In terms of unhealthy cities, Pittsburgh was off the chart.

At that time, Democrats were not a dominant force in Pittsburgh. Lawrence had been elected mayor by only a slim margin, and Republicans still controlled the city. But the new mayor had campaigned on a vow to clean up the air, the water and the blighted downtown, and in this he found an ally in one of the city's leading Republicans, Richard Mellon. The two men were about as opposite in temperament and demeanor as possible, but professionally, they worked together as a team the likes of which is seldom seen today. Mellon created the Allegheny Conference on Community Development. Lawrence proposed the pieces of legislation, and through the conference, Mellon convinced business leaders to go along with them. The mayor put in place emissions controls that, within ten years, reduced pollution to less than 10 percent of what it had been in 1945.

In addition to air pollution controls, Lawrence got business leaders to begin investing in Pittsburgh again. Before he became mayor, several large corporations were threatening to leave because of the air quality and overall squalor of the city. Now, they began to build; prior to 1946, the last major construction downtown had been the Gulf Building in 1932. Lawrence and Mellon again partnered to form the Urban Redevelopment Authority. Bolstered by a fortuitous fire at the Point in 1946, the URA began the process of rebuilding this rundown neighborhood. The outcome was the construction of Gateway Center and the creation of Point State Park.

Although Lawrence has been viewed by many as the savior of Pittsburgh, the charge of "benevolent crook" was not far off the mark. Throughout his career as a politician, which had begun at the age of fourteen when he became a clerk for attorney William Brennan, the chairman of the Democratic Party in the city, Lawrence proved himself to be a shrewd manipulator and a master of the political patronage system. An article in the fall 2010 issue of the *Pittsburgh Quarterly* called the Lawrence political machine a "three-cycle engine": build the Democratic Party, win elections, dispense patronage—and rinse and repeat.

Calling Lawrence a maker of presidents might be generous, but he certainly was a friend and supporter of several of them. From Franklin Delano Roosevelt to Lyndon Baines Johnson, presidents often sought Lawrence's advice and his help, particularly in getting votes for them. When Lawrence died in 1966, President Johnson gave one of the eulogies.

Lawrence's fatal flaw was that he was not an empathetic character. His carrot and stick method might have accomplished an amazing amount of good for Pittsburgh, but it was done in a cold manner, with little regard for its impact on the city's residents. Nowhere was this more evident than in the Hill District in the early 1950s, when the URA condemned much of the lower Hill when it erected the Civic Arena. A comment from City Councilman George Evans echoed Lawrence's own view at the time: "[The Hill] is one of the most outstanding examples in Pittsburgh of neighborhood deterioration. Approximately 90 percent of the buildings in the area are substandard and have long outlived their usefulness. There would be no social loss if they were all destroyed."

The remark about the buildings might have been accurate, but the city was blind about the impact of redevelopment on the community. The URA's plan displaced more than eight thousand residents, and the city didn't have an adequate relocation plan for them. So, the mostly African American citizens simply moved eastward, into the upper Hill, causing more overcrowding and exacerbating an already growing split between blacks and whites. It also signaled the end of the Hill as a jazz mecca.

Despite this miscalculation, Lawrence's four terms as mayor were mostly positive for the city. Cleaner air, cleaner water, a rejuvenated downtown and an influx of new companies and jobs are among his legacy. And yet, the only "memorial" to Lawrence is the convention center named in his honor.

4

MARIO LEMIEUX

THE PENGUIN WHO SAVED PITTSBURGH HOCKEY

*T*o call Mario Lemieux the greatest athlete ever to play in Pittsburgh wouldn't be a stretch. His records speak for themselves: 1,723 points (690 goals, 1,033 assists) in 915 regular season games; Pittsburgh Penguin records for most goals (85) assists (114) and points (199) in a season; second all-time in goals-per-game average (0.75); and two Stanley Cups. He is one of only ten NHL players to be inducted into the Hockey Hall of Fame immediately after retirement, and he is one of only three players to "unretire" after entering the hall. The other two are Guy LaFleur and Gordie Howe.

All this was accomplished in a career interrupted and ultimately cut short by injuries, a bout with Hodgkin's lymphoma and atrial fibrillation. Were it not for these setbacks, Mario's name likely would be above Wayne Gretzky's for many stats, rather than the other way around.

But this is only part of the reason why Mario is so beloved in this town, and it is not the reason he is a Pittsburgh icon. Mario Lemieux is revered in Pittsburgh because he turned around a foundering franchise in 1999 by buying it and turning the Penguins into one of the most successful teams in the NHL.

Mario—which is how virtually everyone in Pittsburgh thinks of him—is a product of Canadian hockey, but he has made Pittsburgh his home. Born in a suburb of Montreal, he was the number one pick in the NHL draft in 1984. Destined for greatness, he wasted little time in making his NHL debut—October 11 of that same year, against the Boston Bruins. He also

Mario Lemieux prepares to drop the ceremonial first puck at Consol Energy Center in 2010. *Wikimedia Commons*.

quickly made his presence felt: during his first shift on the ice, he stole the puck from Ray Bourque, fired a shot at goalie Pete Peeters and scored. He scored 100 points his rookie year and was named rookie of the year. He also became the first rookie to be named MVP of the NHL All-Star Game.

By the 1987–88 season, when Lemieux led the league with 168 points, the Penguins had become a winning team again, for the first time since 1978–79. The following year, with Mario racking up 199 points, the Penguins were a playoff team, and Mario established another first. On New Year's Eve 1988, he became the only player ever to score goals five different ways in one NHL game. Against the New Jersey Devils, he scored at even-strength, on the power play, short-handed, on a penalty shot and into an empty net.

The Penguins won their first Stanley Cup with Lemieux in 1991, beating the Minnesota North Stars. The following year, even with Mario missing sixty-four games, the Penguins again made the playoffs and ultimately defeated the Chicago Blackhawks for consecutive Cup victories.

On January 12, 1993, Lemieux announced that he had been diagnosed with Hodgkin's lymphoma, a type of cancer. In true MVP form, he succeeded in beating the disease, but between the cancer and back problems, he would miss many games over the next three seasons. In 1997, he retired, and later that year, he was inducted into the Hockey Hall of Fame.

Mario would come out of retirement in 2000 and play another six seasons for the Penguins. But what he did the year before he came back would endear him to Pens fans no matter what the future brought. In November 1998, the team had declared bankruptcy. Its owners owed more than $90 million to various creditors, and it seemed likely that the Penguins would either leave the city or fold.

Mario came to the rescue. Because he had deferred salaries in years past to help the team financially, Lemieux was owed $32.5 million—more than any other creditor. He offered to use $20 million of the money as equity, supplemented by $5 million in cash, to gain controlling interest in the club. U.S. Bankruptcy Court, and later the NHL, approved the offer, and Mario became the team's CEO.

Mario made two promises: he would keep the team in Pittsburgh, and he would pay off all the club's debts. The latter was achieved by August 2005. The former, as of 2019, also has been honored; although Lemieux indicated as far back as 2006 that he was willing to sell the team, he has said he would do so only to owners who would agree to keep the Penguins in Pittsburgh. A deal negotiated by Lemieux's organization in 2007 to build a new arena to replace the Civic Arena included a provision that keeps the team in the city until at least 2037.

The Lemieux family has become well established in Pittsburgh. Mario is now a naturalized U.S. citizen, and his family owns a home in the area. In 1993, he created the Mario Lemieux Foundation, which helps fund medical research through its support of groups such as the University of Pittsburgh Cancer Institute, the Leukemia Society and the Lupus Foundation. He is among the founders of Athletes for Hope, which assists professional athletes and non-athletes alike to support their communities through charitable efforts.

"Mario has completely transformed professional hockey history in Pittsburgh," said Anne Madarasz, chief historian at the Heinz History

Center. "He has influenced the popularity of the sport here. He is part of the very conscious effort the Pens have put into developing youth hockey throughout the region, building rinks all around the city. It is something that is continuing with Sidney Crosby.

"We tend to discount the importance of sports here as a business," Madarasz added. "I think that as a businessman, as a philanthropist, as a symbol of the community, he is really like an Arnold Palmer, bigger than the sport itself."

5

FRED ROGERS

A MAN FOR ALL MEDIA

The man best known to millions of young people as Mister Rogers was a multitalented individual. A graduate of Rollins College in Florida with a degree in music composition, he was a musician and a songwriter. After graduating in 1951, he moved to New York City, where he became a floor manager and producer for several TV shows at NBC.

Fred Rogers was a writer—of poetry, scripts, song lyrics and three dozen books, including one for adults titled *Mister Rogers Talks with Parents*. He was a puppeteer, an outgrowth of a childhood in Latrobe, Pennsylvania, often spent alone. It was said that he would use puppets and stuffed animals to create imaginary worlds. This fertile imagination would serve him well in his early days at WQED as part of *Children's Corner* with Josie Carey.

He was, for a time, a publisher. After becoming a vegetarian in the 1970s, he became a co-owner of *Vegetarian Times*.

Rogers was an advocate for children's television and for public broadcasting in general. His testimony in 1969 before the U.S. Senate Subcommittee on Communications regarding funding cuts to public broadcasting is legendary. Largely as a result of his passionate six-minute presentation, not only did Congress not reduce funding, but also, two years later, PBS's government allocation was raised from $9 million to $22 million.

He was an ordained minister in the United Presbyterian Church, having graduated from the Pittsburgh Theological Seminary in 1963. He was also a producer, founding Family Communications Inc.—now the Fred Rogers Company—in 1971 to produce his show along with other programs.

One thing he was not, however, was an actor. At least, not in the sense that he played a role on television. On his Emmy Award–winning *Mister Rogers' Neighborhood*, Fred Rogers was being himself. The kind, gentle, patient, spiritual persona was no act. One of his reasons for becoming involved in television, and why he came to Pittsburgh in late 1953 to become the program director for the new WQED television station, was because he wasn't pleased with the medium. He felt that it wasn't being used to best advantage as an educational tool. At WQED, he set out to change that, and over a thirty-year period, he succeeded tremendously.

When Fred Rogers joined WQED, the station hadn't even gone on the air. Although his title was program director, he learned very quickly that part of his job was going to have to be creating some of the programming. The station's president, Dorothy Daniel, paired him with Josephine Vicari, Daniel's secretary but also a director and actor at the Pittsburgh Playhouse. Daniel changed Vicari's name to Josie Carey. She would be the on-air personality, and Rogers would be the behind-the-scenes puppeteer. The two collaborated on scripts and music for *Children's Corner*, and the show was almost immediately a critical success, winning a Sylvania Award—the precursor to the Emmys—in 1955.

In 1963, Rogers left WQED and Pittsburgh for Toronto and a stint with the Canadian Broadcasting Corporation as the creator and host of *Mister Rogers*. In 1967, he returned to bring his concept of children's programming to Pittsburgh. He had learned much during his time with the CBC. He thought he might reach a larger audience if he took his message to network TV, and so he approached WTAE, Pittsburgh's ABC affiliate, with the idea

Fred Rogers being honored by President George W. Bush in 2002. *Courtesy of the National Archives.*

32

for a fifteen-minute program. Executives at WTAE assigned Joe Negri, the station's musical director, to be Rogers's musical helper.

"We spent six months working together," said Negri. "The problem was, he had to do commercials. He didn't want to do them, and he fought with the sales department. Eventually, he left. A year later he called me and said that he was starting back up."

Rogers had returned to WQED, and his new show would be called *Mister Rogers' Neighborhood*. He asked Negri to join him, not as his musical assistant but as a character, Handyman Negri. Negri said he never found out why he was given that particular character.

"I never could get that [information] out of him," Negri recalled. "But my dad was a very good bricklayer and stonemason by trade, and he could do a little bit of everything. I think Fred picked up on that. When we would go to the Land of Make Believe, King Friday XIII would send me on little chores around the neighborhood."

Mister Rogers' Neighborhood was a much more tightly run operation at WQED than *Children's Corner*. Where the earlier show was very loose and free-flowing, *Neighborhood* was very much a scripted format. Rogers wanted to make sure that the exact message he wanted children to receive got through, Negri said.

"He was a little bit tough when it came to the scripts. He wasn't much for ad-libbing or winging it. You had to stick to what he wrote. He would call in stagehands if you didn't study the script well enough, and they would write the script on big cards and you had to read your lines."

Various people have related that there was only one other thing that would make Fred Rogers grumpy: not getting in his morning swim. It was a daily routine, and missing it could make him irritable. But seeing him that way was a very rare occurrence indeed.

Rogers's messages were mostly about love, accepting yourself and accepting others. But he didn't shy away from uncomfortable subjects: fear, grief, divorce, disabilities, even racism were tackled in the Neighborhood. Sometimes, such as after the terrorist attacks of September 11, 2001, he spoke to parents to help them understand how to talk with their children about what had happened.

He touched people's lives off-screen as well. One memorable event was a wedding ceremony he performed in July 1983. As chronicled by Bob Batz Jr. in the *Pittsburgh Post-Gazette* in 2018, Cathy Tigano was a set designer at WQED, and she was dating a carpenter, Pat Gianella, who also worked at the station. After the couple had been dating for about a year, Gianella proposed to Tigano at the station. Tigano's response was, "I will if you get Fred to marry us." Whether she said it as a joke or not, Gianella took her by the hand, and they went to Rogers's office. Rogers agreed, on one condition: the wedding had to take place that Saturday, or they would have to wait several months. Rogers had a home on Nantucket Island in Massachusetts, and he and his wife, Joanne, were leaving that weekend to spend the rest of the summer there. Tigano and Gianella agreed and were married on the patio of the couple's home on Mount Washington.

During his lifetime, and even after his death in 2003, Fred Rogers has been honored in myriad ways. Aside from the four Emmys *Mister Rogers' Neighborhood* was awarded, Rogers himself received a Lifetime Achievement Award from the Television Academy at the 1997 Daytime Emmy Awards. Two years later, he was inducted into the Television Hall of Fame.

Among the many other honors is the Presidential Medal of Freedom, awarded to him by President George W. Bush in 2002. He has a star on the Hollywood Walk of Fame. Two documentaries about his life have been made, as well as a biopic, starring Tom Hanks, called *A Beautiful Day in the Neighborhood*. His spirit lives on in the educational show *Daniel Tiger's Neighborhood*.

Rogers used to tell people about something his mother would tell him when he encountered disasters and tragic events: "Look for the helpers. You will always find people who are helping." Few people have ever helped children in Pittsburgh—and far beyond—more than did Fred Rogers.

6

ARTHUR J. ROONEY SR.

THE CHIEF

*T*aking a cue from the movie *It's a Wonderful Life*, try to imagine what Pittsburgh's sports history might have been like had Art Rooney Sr. not been born. While it's unlikely that Pittsburgh would never have had a pro football team, it certainly would have been a different team. But Art Rooney had a hand in guiding more than just the Steelers. He was influential in convincing the NHL Board of Governors to grant Pittsburgh a hockey franchise in 1967, and he was part-owner of the team for the first few years of its existence. He also periodically provided financial help to the Homestead Grays baseball team of the Negro League. Had "The Chief" not been there to offer support, Pittsburghers may never have seen one of the greatest baseball players of all time, catcher Josh Gibson.

Most of all, Pittsburgh would never have been blessed with Art Rooney, the man. To anyone who ever knew him, he truly was a special individual. After he died in 1988, Pittsburghers remembered his humility, his passion for the city, his charity and his friendliness. Thomas Foerster, Allegheny County commissioner, called Rooney "our number one citizen. I'm fully convinced he did more for [Pittsburgh] than R.K. Mellon did for the business community and David Lawrence and any of the mayors who followed him…did politically." Pittsburgh mayor Sophie Masloff reminded people that "to Art Rooney, everyone he met was someone special. He made you feel important." NFL commissioner Pete Rozelle told the *New York Times*, "It is questionable whether any sports figure was more universally loved and respected." A memorial plaque at St. Peter's Catholic Church on the

North Side, where Rooney was a parishioner, reads simply, "A man of unfeigned charity."

Rooney came from the quintessential Pittsburgh family. Born in 1901 in Coulterville, Pennsylvania, east of McKeesport, Rooney once explained that his mother's family were all coal miners and his father's family were all steel workers. But when the family moved to Pittsburgh's North Side in 1913, his father, Dan, bought a bar, and the family lived above it. Perhaps Art was always destined to be involved with sports; he lived virtually a stone's throw away from Exposition Park, the original home of the Pittsburgh Pirates baseball club. When the building that housed the bar was torn down in 1969, erected on the site was Three Rivers Stadium, home of the Pirates and the Steelers for three decades.

Art loved sports. He played minor-league baseball and semipro football, and as a boxer he was good enough to try out for the 1920 U.S. Olympics team as a welterweight. He began his sports ownership in the mid-1920s, when he bought the Hope-Harvey football club, for which he was player-manager. He renamed it the J.P. Rooneys.

Art also enjoyed horse racing, and he loved betting on it. Reportedly, it was a win at the track that gave him the $2,500 to buy an NFL franchise for Pittsburgh. (Even though western Pennsylvania is known as "the cradle of professional football," the state's "blue" laws at the time forbade the playing of sports events on Sundays, which was when the NFL's games were scheduled. In 1932, those laws were relaxed enough for Rooney to make his move.)

Rooney called his new team the Pirates because he was a huge baseball fan; the team's name was meant to pay tribute to the city's baseball club. In 1941, he would change the name to the Steelers, because people were becoming confused between the two teams. Again, however, the name was a tribute—this time, to the town known as the "Steel City."

In 1936, Rooney's skill at playing the ponies would help to keep the Steelers in business during lean times. The details have become hazy through the years, but they involve the Empire City racetrack in Yonkers, New York; Rooney's friend Timothy Mara, owner of the New York Giants football team and also a bookmaker; and the track at Saratoga, New York. The story goes that Rooney asked Mara to "pick a winner" for Rooney. How much Rooney bet isn't certain, but the point is that bet was placed on something of a longshot, which won and netted Rooney somewhere north of $1,500. The next day, Rooney took his winnings up to Saratoga, and when the dust settled, he had won more than $300,000.

The Chief with his four Super Bowl trophies. *Pittsburgh Steelers.*

It is ironic that, under the rules of the league today, neither Rooney nor Mara would be allowed to own an NFL franchise because of their gambling ties. But back then, not only did Art Rooney bet on the ponies, he also owned racetracks. At one time or another, he owned Yonkers Raceway in New York and the Liberty Bell Park Racetrack near Philadelphia, as well as Shamrock Stables in Maryland.

A young Arthur J. Rooney. *Pittsburgh Steelers.*

Over the years, Art and the Rooney family often brushed shoulders with the wealthy and the famous, just in the course of doing business. Sometimes, though, they had the good fortune of being involved with athletes long before they became people of note. When Art won his money at Saratoga, one of the things he spent it on was a contract for a young running back from Notre Dame, Byron "Whizzer" White. Years later, White would find himself on a different type of "bench"—as a justice of the U.S. Supreme Court. Then, his son Dan, as a young man, coached the St. Peter's Elementary School football team. Among his players was a quarterback by the name of Michael Hayden. Hayden would grow up to become a four-star general in the U.S. Air Force and, from 2006 to 2009, director of the Central Intelligence Agency.

Today, Art Rooney lives on as a member of the Pro Football Hall of Fame and as one of the *Sporting News*' "100 Most Powerful Sports Figures of the 20th Century." Twelve years after his death, he was inducted into the American Football Association's Semi-Pro Football Hall of Fame. Duquesne University's football field is named in his honor, as is the street that runs alongside Heinz Field, the Steelers' current home. Because, when you are larger than life, your spirit can never die.

7

MARY SCHENLEY

UNCONVENTIONAL PHILANTHROPIST

Schenley is one of the most well-known names in Pittsburgh. It is attached to the city's second-largest park, a plaza and fountain in the Oakland section of the city and a high school in the Hill District. Until 1956, it was also the name of one of the most luxurious hotels in Pittsburgh. Tourists and new residents might incorrectly assume that the name is that of one of the city's great male philanthropists, like Carnegie, Frick or Mellon. But Mary Schenley was without a doubt the city's most unusual benefactor. First, philanthropy among women in the nineteenth century was rare. Second, Schenley nearly lost her fortune before she was even old enough to control it because of a youthful indiscretion.

Mary Elizabeth Croghan was born in 1826 outside of Louisville, Kentucky, to William and Mary O'Hara Croghan. Mary Elizabeth's mother was the daughter of James O'Hara, during the Revolutionary War the quartermaster general of the Continental army, under General George Washington. O'Hara became an enterprising Pittsburgh businessman who invested in a number of industries, as well as in real estate. When O'Hara died in 1819, his daughter inherited his vast estate.

A few months after Mary Elizabeth's birth, Mary O'Hara Croghan died. A year later, Mary Elizabeth's older brother William also died. So, before she was even two years old, Mary Elizabeth was suddenly the largest landowner in Allegheny County. She and her father moved to Pittsburgh, where he began practicing law. He built a twenty-two-room mansion in Stanton Heights, where Mary lived until she was nine. Then, as was the

Young Mary Schenley. *Sarah H. Killikelly*, The History of Pittsburgh: Its Rise and Progress.

custom among wealthy families, Mary was sent to a "finishing" school to continue her education. This particular school was Mrs. McLeod's School on Staten Island, outside New York City, run by Richmond Margaret McLeod and attended by a number of the daughters of Pittsburgh's elite.

When Mary was fifteen, she was introduced to Captain Edward W. Schenley, the brother-in-law of McLeod. Schenley, a forty-three-year-old British army officer, was a handsome gentleman, a decorated hero of the Napoleonic Wars and apparently quite the ladies' man. He courted young Mary for a year, and the couple was married in secret on January 22, 1842. For Mary, this was like a magical dream. For Captain Schenley, it was simply his third marriage, all of them by elopement. For William Croghan, it was literally a stroke-inducing nightmare.

The scandal had far-reaching repercussions. Reportedly, Queen Victoria refused to receive them at court. Newspapers and politicians denounced Captain Schenley as a callous fortune-hunter. McLeod was disgraced; several Pittsburgh families pulled their daughters out of the school, which eventually had to close. Schenley, who had been absent without leave from the British army throughout the courtship, was ordered back to his post, which was in British Guiana. The colony's main source of income was the slave trade. Schenley's position was as Her Majesty's Commissioner of Arbitration in a court for the suppression of the slave trade. The job was fairly short-lived; slave owners were so vehemently opposed to Schenley's attempts to free slaves that the couple's lives were threatened to the point where they had to flee the colony.

When Croghan recovered from his mild stroke, he beseeched the Pennsylvania legislature to cede him control over his daughter's landholdings. The subsequent bill "confirms the title of the whole of the property to the father of Miss Crogan [*sic*]…and places the same after his death in the hands of trustees who are to pay at their discretion for her support." So, if Schenley had indeed married Mary for her fortune, he was now out of luck.

But William Croghan's anger could not outweigh the love he had for his only surviving child. A couple of years later, Croghan visited the Schenleys in England. He forgave his daughter and accepted his son-in-law. He bought them a new home in London and even replicated the home in Pittsburgh as an addition to his mansion. He hoped that the gesture would convince the Schenleys to move back to the States.

The Schenleys would visit Pittsburgh twice while Croghan was alive. There are varying reports concerning why the Schenleys chose to stay in England. Some people believe that Mary, being asthmatic, couldn't handle the polluted Pittsburgh air. Others say that Captain Schenley opposed the move, considering life in the United States to be "too primitive" for his tastes. The Schenleys, who had seven children, lived in England until his death in 1889.

When William Croghan died in 1850, Mary Schenley finally received her inheritance; it was valued at $50 million. Between then and her death in 1903, Mary Schenley made several sizeable donations to the city, such as land for the site of West Penn Hospital, the Western Pennsylvania School for Blind Children and the Pittsburgh Newsboys Home.

In 1889, Schenley made her greatest gift to the city, the 425-acre park that bears her name. Although city officials had coveted the land for decades, it wasn't until a land developer expressed interest that they acted on their desires. Edward Manning Bigelow, Pittsburgh's director of public works and also its parks commissioner, had been fighting for years to develop parks in the city. As the city grew, Bigelow feared that developers would gobble up all the available land for housing, businesses and factories. So, when he discovered that one of these developers was planning a trip to England to meet with Mary Schenley, he dispatched his own emissary, a lawyer who managed to arrive before the developer. He explained Bigelow's desire for a park, and Mary agreed to donate 300 acres of land in Oakland. She made only two demands: the park would be named after her, and the land could never be sold. She also gave the city the option to purchase an additional 100 acres, which it did for $125,000.

Mary Schenley's other real estate dealings included the donation of the Fort Pitt Blockhouse to the Daughters of the American Revolution, the land for the Carnegie Institute and the land upon which the Cathedral of Learning at the University of Pittsburgh now stands. Inside that skyscraper can be found the Croghan-Schenley Ballroom and Oval Room, the last surviving rooms of William Croghan's mansion. The rooms were donated in 1955 by William S. Miller, president of the Steelwood Corporation, who had purchased the mansion as a site for a new housing development. The rooms were taken apart and rebuilt inside the first floor of the Cathedral of Learning. They were redone in 1982.

In 1918, the city decided to erect a monument to Mary Schenley. Sculptor Victor David Brenner designed a bronze statue above a granite fountain created by architect Harold Van Buren Magonigle. It stands at the entrance to Schenley Park. Called *A Song to Nature*, the artwork features the Greek god Pan sitting below a female playing a lyre. Below the statues rests a bowl, from which four turtles spew water. The entire sculpture is thirty feet tall and bears an inscription that reads, "A Song of Nature, Pan the Earth God Answers to the Harmony and Magic Tones Sung to the Lyre by Sweet Humanity."

8

DR. THOMAS STARZL

TRANSPLANT GURU

Dr. Thomas E. Starzl wasn't born here, didn't grow up here, didn't even spend most of his life here. But much like Andrew Carnegie and David Lawrence, he helped transform this city—in his case, making Pittsburgh the transplantation capital of the world and a leading center for immunological therapy.

What Starzl accomplished in his thirty-six years in Pittsburgh was not only to prove that liver transplants could be performed successfully, but also to lead the effort to develop the drug therapies that would prevent bodies from rejecting transplanted organs—not only livers—to dramatically improve the success rate.

"He was a visionary," said the Heinz History Center's Anne Madarasz. "He wasn't just a surgeon who came and brought his surgical skills. He was someone who had to figure out an experimental procedure and make it a clinical procedure."

When Starzl came to the University of Pittsburgh Medical Center from Boulder, Colorado, in 1981, he brought with him a reputation as a man obsessed with accomplishing the impossible and possessing a work ethic that would put most hardworking Pittsburghers to shame. It's interesting that Starzl's father was a writer of science fiction, because that's what many other doctors thought Starzl's work was. Since 1963, he had been attacking the problem of how to successfully transplant organs from one person to another. Kidney transplants had become fairly common since the 1950s, but Starzl was struggling with the problem of rejection: organs were being attacked by their new hosts, and even when anti-rejection drugs were successful, the side effects could be devastating.

In 1979, Starzl helped develop a new drug—cyclosporine—and tested it successfully on human transplant patients. Success rates rose dramatically, but even so, the first four liver transplants he performed in Pittsburgh were failures. He was attacked by colleagues and journalists. One famous exchange occurred in 1983 on the ABC program *Nightline* involving Starzl, Surgeon General Dr. C. Everett Koop and journalist Ted Koppel. Koppel kept hammering away at the failure rate of transplant surgeries, accusing Starzl of giving patients "false hope"—even as Starzl pointed out that the failure rate without surgery was 100 percent.

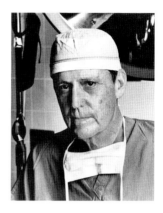

Dr. Tom Starzl in his surgical scrubs. *Courtesy of Historic Pittsburgh.*

Carl Kurlander, co-producer of a documentary about Starzl's work, once told *Cleveland Magazine*: "For Dr. Starzl, it was never a job. It was a mission. It was painstaking. He always ignored the bullets because he had a confidence in his vision."

The transplant challenge involved much more than simply organ failure or the body's rejection of the organ. Said Madarasz: "Look at what he had to do to make that transplant possible. He had to figure out how to keep the liver alive. How do you transport it safely? He built an entire transportation system to make this possible in Pittsburgh."

Indeed, Starzl convinced several Pittsburgh corporations to make their corporate jets available on very short notice to help transport organs to UPMC—the window from harvesting the organ to transplanting it was very narrow. Starzl was often quick to credit Pittsburghers' efforts in helping his transplant work succeed.

In 1984, Starzl achieved perhaps his greatest success to date when he performed a heart-liver transplant on six-year-old Stormie Jones of Fort Worth, Texas. Stormie suffered from a rare condition in which the body's LDL cholesterol is elevated to near-lethal levels. When she came to Children's Hospital needing a new liver, doctors determined that because she had already had a double bypass operation—the result of two recent heart attacks—her heart would not be strong enough to survive the liver transplant. So, using the heart and liver of a four-year-old New York City girl who died in an auto accident, Starzl transplanted both organs. Stormie Jones lived for seven years after the procedure, until her body unexpectedly rejected the heart.

Starzl was much more than a surgeon performing a difficult procedure. He was also, in several ways, a caregiver as well. "Many people don't realize how actively involved he was in determining and handling the whole regimen of patient care," Madarasz noted. "He developed a lifelong relationship with his patients. He also was very involved in medical ethics, the ethics of transplantation."

Starzl retired from surgery in 1991, but he remained active on the immunological side. Two years earlier, he and his team had successfully tried a new anti-rejection drug known as FK506. This breakthrough improved survival rates, not only for liver transplant patients but also for those involving hearts, lungs and other organs. Then, in 1992, he discovered that rejection was not always guaranteed without drug therapy. He found that some recipients' bodies do accept their new organs. So, it was possible to wean people off anti-rejection drugs and allow their bodies to learn to bond with the new organ. Other research has shown that this is likely true for less than one-third of all transplants, but for those few, the risks of serious side effects from long-term immunotherapy are greatly reduced.

Starzl's research has spread around the world. According to the Institute for Scientific Information, between 1981 and 1998, Starzl had been cited in other medical journals and research papers more than twenty-six thousand times—more than any other researcher in the world. Some people believe that his research was in many ways more valuable than the transplant surgery he perfected.

Starzl died in 2017, but his name lives on in Oakland through the Thomas E. Starzl Transplantation Institute, so named in 1996, and the Thomas E. Starzl Biomedical Science Tower, renamed in 2006. In 2007, at the request of the Western Pennsylvania American Liver Foundation, the city dedicated Lothrop Street, on the campus of UPMC Medical Center, as Thomas E. Starzl Way.

9

ANDY WARHOL

POP ICON

*I*t would be easy to think that Andy Warhol, an artist who became famous only after leaving his hometown of Pittsburgh and moving to New York City, has had no more influence on this city than any other celebrity whose ties to Pittsburgh are only through birth. But spend a day at the Andy Warhol Museum on Sandusky Street on the city's North Side, and you will view the pop artist in an entirely different light.

"It blows my mind to walk through the museum and see so many people enjoying it," says Donald Warhola, Andy's nephew, Warhola family historian and vice president of the Andy Warhol Foundation for the Visual Arts. "I think it's done Pittsburgh a lot of good, having the museum here."

John Warhola, Andy's brother and Donald's father, was one of the driving forces behind the seven-floor museum, which opened in 1994. In 1989, when the Dia Art Foundation and the Warhol Foundation decided to open a museum dedicated to the artist, John lobbied hard for the museum to be located in Pittsburgh. The Carnegie Foundation agreed to provide the building, and the Warhol Foundation supplied the art.

"When the museum opened, I was wondering what we were going to do with all that space," said Warhola. "Now, I think they could use another seven floors; my uncle was just so prolific in his work."

But the museum is only part of Andy Warhol's legacy. The larger, but less visible, aspect is the Warhol Foundation, which was established in 1987, after the artist's untimely death from complications from gall bladder surgery. Andy stipulated in his will that virtually all of his estate was to be liquidated

One room at the Andy Warhol Museum contains more than three hundred boxes of items collected by the artist during his lifetime. *Photo by author.*

to fund the foundation, which was charged with doing everything in its power to advance the visual arts. And it was, as it turned out, a vast estate; it took Sotheby's ten days to auction off Andy's collectables and antiques, generating more than $20 million.

According to its website, the foundation's goal "is to foster innovative artistic expression and the creative process by encouraging and supporting cultural organizations that in turn, directly or indirectly, support artists and their work. The foundation is focused primarily on supporting work of a challenging and often experimental nature, while noting that the interpretation of those terms may vary from place to place and culture to culture. In this regard the Foundation encourages curatorial research leading to new scholarship in the field of contemporary art." Warhola explained that the money often goes to museums or art programs in smaller cities, places that otherwise might not have the funds to support such programs. Most recently, in the spring of 2019, the foundation awarded $3.81 million to forty-one artist-focused foundations.

In this regard, the foundation's mission fits very well with the narrative of Andy Warhol's life, which was to take the side of the underdog—perhaps, his uncle said, because Andy was "an underdog himself." He was born in Pittsburgh in 1927 to Andrej and Julia Warhola, Eastern European immigrants. When he was about nine years old, Andy contracted a nervous disorder that sometimes confined him to bed. During those times, he developed both his art and his love for celebrities. His parents saw great potential in him, so much so that Andrej had set aside $1,500 in savings bonds for college by the time Andy was thirteen. Before Andrej died, after drinking what was believed to be tainted spring water, he told John, Andy's older brother, that it was now his responsibility to take care of Andy and make sure that his brother went to college. "He told my dad, 'you are going to be proud of him one day,'" Warhola recalled.

Julia, an artist in her own right, was just as supportive. She and an art teacher convinced Andy to enter a citywide art contest in 1943. The prize was a series of art classes. Andy won the event and was set on his career path. He graduated from Schenley High School in 1945 and attended Carnegie Tech to study pictorial design. After graduation, he set out for the Big Apple to become a commercial artist.

Even though Andy Warhol is best known for his celebrity portraits of people such as Marilyn Monroe, and for his Campbell's Soup can series, there is plenty of artwork that demonstrated Andy's attitude toward those who may have been disassociated from the world at large.

"He never missed opportunities to reach out and represent the marginalized in society," said his nephew. "His drag queen series, in the early '70s, is a perfect example of that. Back then they were seen as strange and different. But my uncle painted them in portraits and gave them the same care and technique and quality that he used on celebrities. His message was, 'These are beautiful people and this is how I see them.'"

This attitude also explains his willingness, in 1983, to create an art exhibition for children. Bruno Bischofberger, a Zurich, Switzerland art dealer, had complained to Warhol that when he took his kids to a museum, he had to hold them up to see the artwork. So Warhol did a series of 128 images of toys, animals and circus clowns. The paintings were hung at child height in the Bischofberger Gallery, which debuted the exhibition on December 3, 1983, to great success.

"The children's art was a bold move," said Warhola. "Other artists might have said, 'these kids aren't going to buy my art.' But that was Uncle Andy being human."

That spirit lives on today through the museum, which has a partnership with an organization called the Caring Place. This group works with children who have lost loved ones.

One artist to another: Andy Warhol conversing with playwright Tennessee Williams. *Library of Congress.*

"The families come here and they learn the story of Andy Warhol, of how his father died when he was 13, how he almost died in his 40s, and how, when his mother died in 1972, he memorialized her with a portrait," explained Donald Warhola. "Then we go down to the studio [in the basement of the museum] and they take digitized images of loved ones they have lost and produce portraits on T-shirts, on paper, on notebooks—whatever they want. It's a great way to bring Andy Warhol's story into people's lives, and a way they can gain some healing and inspiration."

Warhol is best known as a painter and a sculptor, but there was much more of an artistic nature that he was involved with. He was a prolific filmmaker, and he was a publisher, founding *Interview* magazine in 1969. He was also a collector and a pack rat. After his death, it was discovered that he had, in his apartment and in a storage space, more than six hundred "time capsules"—boxes that contained everything from artwork to airplane menus. The boxes are on view at the museum, behind glass in a special room.

that trains had two major problems; braking was a difficult process, and trains had a tendency to "jump" the tracks.

In 1866, George Westinghouse solved the first problem by inventing a device that could reseat derailed train cars. Prior to this, trainmen had to move cars back onto the tracks using crowbars, a process that could take hours. He followed this invention with the "frog." With the help of two Schenectady, New York men who were friends of his father's, George formed his first company.

Problems with his business partners—they reportedly wanted Westinghouse to sell his patents to them—sent Westinghouse searching for new partners and manufacturers. He traveled to Pittsburgh, which had earned its reputation as a center for iron and steel manufacturing, and he partnered with the Anderson & Cook Foundry to produce his switches.

In Pittsburgh, he turned his attention to the braking problem and soon came up with a solution: an air brake, in which a compressor feeds air through a pipe into air tanks on each car. Applying the brakes would force air into the pipes and push the brake pads against the drum. Westinghouse created the Westinghouse Air Brake Company in 1869 to sell his new invention while working to improve it—which he did with the triple-valve air brake system.

He also worked on the challenge of signaling trains and switching them from one track to another, inventing a signal device that used both compressed air and electricity. In 1881, he formed the Union Switch and Signal Company. Using his inventions and the patents of other inventors, the company greatly improved this system for railroads. Westinghouse made advances in two other industries in his lifetime: electricity and natural gas. The former brought him into contact—and conflict—with Thomas Edison.

In Edison's experiments with electricity, he believed that direct current was the best way to transmit this energy. In direct current, the electricity flows in one direction. It had its limits, in terms of how far the current could travel. But some scientists argued that it was safer than alternating current, in which the flow switches directions back and forth. It had been proven that alternating current, with the ability to be increased to very high voltages, could travel farther. The catch? Alternating current needed transformers to reduce the voltage so it could be used by homes and businesses. For this reason, Edison and others believed alternating current was too dangerous to use.

Westinghouse set out to prove the direct current adherents wrong. In 1884, he formed the Westinghouse Electric Company and bought the rights to a patent on a transformer developed by two Europeans. In 1888, he gained sole rights to Nikola Tesla's patents for a new system of transmitting alternating current and convinced Tesla to join him in his quest to perfect this system.

In 1893, Westinghouse and Tesla got their chance to demonstrate the efficiency and safety of alternating current. Westinghouse Electric won the bid to provide all the lighting for the Chicago World's Fair. Later that year, Westinghouse Electric won a contract to design three large generators at Niagara Falls to generate electricity. Within three years, the city of Buffalo was being powered by hydroelectricity, and alternating current had proven its superiority to direct current. By the beginning of the twentieth century, alternating current was being used to power the New York City subway system and locomotives on the New York, New Haven and Hartford Railroad.

Portrait of George Westinghouse, taken by Joseph Gessford sometime after 1900. *Library of Congress.*

Westinghouse's final major contribution was the development of a safe system for conveying natural gas. Natural gas was easily gotten in western Pennsylvania; there was even a vein of it running underneath Westinghouse's home in the Point Breeze section of the city. In 1884, the vein was tapped and natural gas came spewing out of Westinghouse's backyard. After capping the well, he worked on the challenge of transporting the gas through pipes. He formed yet another company, the Philadelphia Company, and over the next two years, he invented nearly thirty new items, all dealing with some aspect of the transmission system. Natural gas could now replace coal as the preferred fuel source for the nation.

During his career, Westinghouse demonstrated his skill as an inventor, and he also showed scientific and business savvy in recognizing the value of other people's inventions and making use of them. He was also a rare individual for the era: a compassionate industrialist. Westinghouse believed that money did not have to be made by exploiting workers. His companies were among the first to institute nine-hour workdays and limit work weeks to fifty-five hours—a long work schedule by today's standards but noteworthy at a time when many companies were forcing employees to work as many as twelve hours a day.

At the height of his success, Westinghouse employed more than fifty thousand people, and his companies were worth a combined $120 million. But the Panic of 1907 caused him to lose control of his companies. However, his legacy was secured by the time he died of a heart condition in 1914— just six years before Westinghouse Electric and KDKA would make radio history.

11

AUGUST WILSON

PLAYWRIGHT LAUREATE

August Wilson is not just one of the greatest writers to come out of Pittsburgh. Wilson is one of the best playwrights this nation has ever seen. The awards speak for themselves: two Pulitzer Prizes, a Tony Award, Artist of the Year (*Chicago Tribune*, 1987) and numerous other awards from organizations such as the New York Drama Critics' Circle and the Outer Critics Circle. Posthumously, he was voted into the American Theater Hall of Fame (2008), he earned an Oscar nomination in 2016 when his play *Fences* was made into a movie and his play *Jitney* won a Tony Award in 2017 for Best Revival of a Play. All told, that's not bad for a kid who never graduated high school.

Wilson, born Frederick August Kittel Jr. in 1945, was the son of a German immigrant baker and Daisy Wilson, a North Carolina native who was a house cleaner. Kittel Sr. wasn't very involved in his children's lives—August was one of six—and Daisy raised the kids alone in a two-room apartment above a grocery store on Bedford Avenue in the Hill District. When August was about ten, his mother divorced Kittel and married David Bedford, then moved out of the Hill and into Oakland.

As a teenager, Wilson spent time in three high schools but never really fit in. As a freshman at Central Catholic High School, he was one of only a dozen or so African American students, and he left after a year because of the racial hatred he encountered. He transferred to Connelley Vo-Tech High School, but he became bored with the curriculum, so he enrolled at Gladstone High School in Hazelwood. There, he was accused by a teacher of plagiarism. Insulted, he left Gladstone before he had finished his sophomore year.

Although he didn't tell his mother, Wilson never attended school again. He started working a variety of jobs, and his spare time was spent at the Carnegie Library in Oakland—he believed he learned more from reading than he could from spending time in classrooms. He spent so much time there in his mid-teens that he convinced library officials to give him a diploma, which they did in 1989.

Wilson loved to write, and he began with poetry. That morphed into playwriting, and in 1968, he and Rob Penny cofounded the Black Horizon Theater. It was through this association that he was able to see his first play, *Recycling*, performed. From that beginning, he would write more than a dozen plays in a career that took him from Pittsburgh to St. Paul, Minnesota, then to Seattle, Washington, where he died in 2005 from liver cancer.

Wilson's legacy is a series of ten plays, nine of which are set in the Hill District, that makes up what is called The Pittsburgh Cycle. The plays span the twentieth century, each one set in a different decade. The plays were not written in chronological order—the first, *Jitney*, is set in the 1970s; the last, *Radio Golf*, takes place in the 1990s—and they are only loosely connected by certain characters who appear in more than one play. But they do follow a basic theme, that of the black experience in the twentieth century. Wilson summed up the theme to George Plimpton and Bonnie Lyons for a 1999 article that appeared in the *Paris Review*: "I once wrote a short story called 'The Best Blues Singer in the World,' and it went like this: 'The streets that Balboa walked were his own private ocean, and Balboa was drowning.' End of story….I've been rewriting that same story over and over again. All my plays are rewriting that same story."

The Pittsburgh Cycle consists of, in the order in which he wrote them, *Jitney* (1970s), *Ma Rainey's Black Bottom* (1920s), *Joe Turner's Come and Gone* (1910s), *Fences* (1950s), *The Piano Lesson* (1930s), *Two Trains Running* (1960s), *Seven Guitars* (1940s), *King Hedley II* (1980s), *Gem of the Ocean* (1900s) and *Radio Golf* (1990s). Although all ten have played on Broadway, only two theaters have staged all of them: the Seattle Repertory Theater and The Actors' Group in Honolulu.

Wilson was a strong-willed man, which stirred controversy from time to time. In staging his plays, he insisted on hiring black actors and black directors. He said he based his decision "not on the basis of race but on the basis of culture"—his plays were about the struggles and experiences of the black community, and Wilson felt that only people who have lived those experiences could adequately portray them.

This opinion most famously caused Wilson grief when Hollywood came knocking. A studio wanted to do a film version of *Fences*. Wilson agreed, on the condition that a black director be hired for the film. The studio balked, and Wilson never saw the film produced. Ten years after his death, however, it was shot—with Denzel Washington directing. It received four Academy Award nominations, including Wilson for Best Adapted Screenplay and Viola Davis (who won) for Best Supporting Actress.

Today, Wilson is remembered in various ways all across the country. Shortly after his death, the Virginia Theater on Broadway was renamed the August Wilson Theater. There is a street named after him near the Seattle Repertory Theater. And in Pittsburgh, there is the August Wilson Cultural Center. His childhood home on Bedford Avenue has been designated a Pennsylvania Historical Landmark and placed on the list of the City of Pittsburgh's historical designations, and Duquesne University students have been working since 2011 to refurbish the house. In addition, the university has partnered with the Nancy Jones Beard Foundation to establish an August Wilson House Fellowship. Selected fellows will serve as artists/scholars in residence while they teach, do research and participate in educational events while working on their own creative projects.

PART II

Places

12

CATHEDRAL OF LEARNING

MONUMENT TO EDUCATION

or more than eighty years, the Cathedral of Learning has stood on the campus of the University of Pittsburgh as a monument to education and a landmark visible for miles. People driving in from the east often catch sight of it before any other building in the city. The Gothic Revival structure stands 535 feet tall, and early in its construction, it was the tallest building in the city. Before it could be finished, in 1934, the Gulf Building downtown eclipsed it in height.

The Cathedral of Learning was conceived in 1921 by John Gabbert Bowman, the university's chancellor. Bowman thought the university needed a symbol of its mission as a developer of minds and that, as a symbol, it should be big. He chose fourteen acres of land, alternately known as Frick Acres or Schenley Farms, which was part of the land Mary Schenley had deeded to the city in 1898. Bowman asked the Mellon family to intercede on his behalf, and they convinced the city to give the plot to the university.

Bowman hired architect Charles Klauder to design the building, and when Klauder and Bowman unveiled the plans, the local community—including some university personnel—was aghast. Where the two men saw a beautiful monument, residents saw a sore thumb; the building was simply too tall for the area, they believed. (Even after it was finished, not everyone was impressed. Frank Lloyd Wright reportedly once called the building "the most stupendous keep-off-the-grass sign I've ever seen.")

Bowman was undeterred. He set about winning people over by involving them in the project. In 1925, the year before ground was broken on the site, he invited schoolchildren to "Buy a Brick for Pitt." Kids were asked to mail in a dime, along with a letter explaining how they had earned the money, to the university. A total of ninety-seven thousand kids participated, each of them receiving a certificate showing that they had purchased a brick. In addition, seventeen thousand other individuals made donations. But corporations made up the bulk of the contributions, not only of money but also of materials, such as steel, cement and glass. The building was ready for classes in 1931, its exterior was completed in 1934 and "Cathy," as it is sometimes called, was dedicated in 1937. By then, Pittsburghers had warmed to the monolith.

But as impressive as the finished structure was, what was added inside would prove to be Bowman's best legacy. As ground was being broken in 1926, the chancellor conceived of a way to demonstrate the diverse influence immigrants have had on the city. He invited each ethnic group represented in the city to design, decorate and furnish one room in the tower. These "nationality rooms" were to reflect life in each country or region at a time before 1787, the year in which Pitt was founded.

Ruth Crawford Mitchell was appointed to interact with the city's ethnic groups, helping them to form Room Committees that would be totally responsible for their rooms, from fundraising to completion. When rooms were finished, the university took them over, agreeing to maintain them "in perpetuity." However, the committees' involvement wouldn't end there. They would arrange cultural events and exchanges and continue to raise money for scholarships that would support students' study-abroad programs.

The committees were given some specific instructions regarding the design and content of their rooms. Among them were that the rooms depict the architectural and design traditions of a particular era in the country's history. Any period prior to 1787 was acceptable, so visitors touring the Nationality Rooms will find designs ranging from sixteenth-century German Renaissance to classical Greek design of the fifth century BC. The rooms are all cultural in nature; no political symbols are allowed, and no images of people currently alive can be displayed.

Each project would prove to be a long-term effort. It took committees from three to ten years to acquire materials—often with the help of the countries' governments—and to design and construct the room. The first four rooms were dedicated in 1938. They were the German, Russian, Scottish and Swedish Rooms. Later that same year came the Early American Room, while Chinese, Czechoslovak, Hungarian and Yugoslav Rooms followed in 1939. (The Early American Room was not meant to be a Nationality

Pitt's Cathedral of Learning, the second-tallest university building in the world. *Photo by author.*

Room. Located on the second floor, it was part of a proposal for a series of "Pennsylvania" rooms. However, only the one room was built, and so it was simply added to the list of Nationality Rooms.)

Mitchell remained the Nationality Room program director until 1956 and has nineteen dedicated rooms to her credit. When she retired, the program stagnated until 1965, when E. Maxine Bruhns was appointed director. Under her guidance, eleven new rooms have been added, the most recent being the Korean Room in 2015. Three more rooms are currently being developed: Finnish, Iranian and Philippine. Two more—Moroccan and Thai—have been proposed, and that presents a problem. Pitt's provost has capped the number of rooms at thirty-three, which will be met when the Philippine Room is dedicated. (As of early 2019, Bruhls, at the age of ninety-one, was still director. She had been quoted as saying she would fight to at least get the Moroccan Room added.)

Twenty-eight of the thirty rooms are still used as classrooms, while the other two are for special events only. But since 1944, when the rooms are not in use, they have been made available for tours. An average of 100,000 people visit the rooms each year, 60 percent of them taking self-guided tours. Groups making reservations are guided by Pitt students who are members of an organization called Quo Vadis. The Nationality Room committees are still active, and they report on news and events related to their specific spaces in a quarterly magazine called *Nationality and Heritage Room News*.

There is, of course, much more to the Cathedral of Learning than the Nationality Rooms. There is the four-story-high, vault-ceilinged Commons Room on the main floor, which covers half an acre of ground. Its walls are Indiana limestone, and its floor is made of Vermont slate. There is the Croghan-Schenley Ballroom and the Oval Room, which were originally in William Croghan Jr.'s mansion in Stanton Heights. In 1955, the rooms were dismantled, transported to the Cathedral and rebuilt. (There are people who believe that, when the rooms were brought to the Cathedral, the ghost of Mary Schenley came with them and that she wanders the lower floors of the building.)

Finally, there is the exterior of the building itself, undoubtedly the most photographed building on campus. It is the second-tallest building on a college campus in the world. It has a steel frame covered over with Indiana limestone, with vertical, parallel lines that convey Bowman's message that learning is never-ending.

13

FORBES FIELD

A PARK AHEAD OF ITS TIME

Not all of Pittsburgh's structural icons are still standing. The Civic Arena, gone since 2011, is a prime example of a building that lives on only in the memories of many Pittsburghers. But there is an entire generation of Yinzers who have no recollection of an even more impressive icon, one that set the bar for sports facilities shortly after the turn of the last century.

Forbes Field stood in Oakland for more than sixty years as the home of the Pittsburgh Pirates baseball club. Opened on June 30, 1909, for a game against the defending World Series champion Chicago Cubs, Forbes Field was unique at the time. It was the first ballpark to be constructed out of steel and concrete and featured a two-tiered grandstand (a third tier was added in 1938), luxury suites and ramps to take fans from one level to the next. It cost between $1 million and $2 million to build and could seat twenty-three thousand spectators. But on the warm, sunny afternoon that marked its opening, more than thirty thousand fans crowded into Forbes Field, with people sitting on the outfield walls and standing in the aisles.

Barney Dreyfuss, president of the ball club, called the day "the happiest day of my life," as he probably felt no small measure of satisfaction. When he bought the land on which the ballpark would stand, critics called his plan "Dreyfuss's Folly." Many people felt the site was too far away from downtown Pittsburgh to attract many fans. Dreyfuss, for his part, wanted to move away from the Allegheny River, where Exposition Park, the Pirates' home, was located, because it often flooded.

Dreyfuss had faith and money, and the land he purchased with the help of Andrew Carnegie was cheap. The inexpensive price allowed him to spend more of his money on the ballpark itself, and he believed that it was only a matter of time before the city would spread out to engulf the neighborhoods surrounding the structure. He was right, and by the time construction began on Forbes Field, there were very few public critics. The ballpark was so successful that, in 1925, its capacity was increased to forty-one thousand.

The architect was Charles Wellford Leavitt Jr., and he brought his experience using streel and concrete on New York's Belmont and Saratoga horse-racing tracks to bear in following Dreyfuss's conception of the facility. Fred Clarke, the manager of the Pirates in 1909, added his two cents, and they were valuable: he designed and patented a device that would allow grounds crews to cover the infield with a canvas tarp when it rained.

Forbes Field was a monster of a ballpark. The outfield wall in left field stood 360 feet from home plate—and that was the shortest distance to the stands. The right-field line was 376 feet away; straightaway center was 442 feet away. The farthest point was in left-center field, an astounding 462 feet away. As if that weren't enough of a challenge for home run hitters, the outfield wall in 1909 was 12 feet high.

View up the left-field line at old Forbes Field. *Library of Congress.*

Forbes Field could be a strange place to play baseball. For starters, the infield was rock-hard, and balls could take strange bounces. Bob Prince, the Pirates' colorful radio announcer from 1948 to 1975, dubbed the ground "alabaster plaster." Outfielders had their own set of challenges. Near the outfield wall were a flagpole and two light towers; all three were in play. In addition, the Pirates would "store" the pregame batting cage along the wall near the 457-foot sign, with the fencing facing home plate. With all these "distractions," it is no wonder that the park was famous for triples and inside-the-park home runs—in one game, the Pirates hit eight triples. In more than 4,700 games over sixty years, no pitcher ever threw a no-hitter at Forbes Field.

Frank O'Donnell, native Pittsburgher and amateur baseball historian, explained that the park's playing field was designed to maximize run production during what was known as the "dead ball" era.

"Players didn't hit many home runs back then," O'Donnell said. "Teams played 'inside baseball' playing for one run at a time. Larger outfields promoted doubles and triples, and if there were large crowds, rope was strung in front of the walls in the outfield where fans would pay to stand to watch the game. Owen 'Chief' Wilson, playing for the Pirates in 1912, hit 36 triples—a record that probably never will be broken. Players don't hit 36 triples in their careers now."

During a renovation in 1925, when stands were added in right field, the right-field line was reduced to 330 feet and the wall was shortened to 9 feet. Dreyfuss countered this, however, by placing a 28-foot-high screen atop the wall. Outfield dimensions were altered for various reasons over the years, and by the time the park closed in 1970, they ranged from 300 feet down the right-field line to 457 feet in the deepest part of center field.

In its inaugural season, Forbes Field helped usher in the Pirates' first World Series win. Pittsburgh would go on to win two more Series there; in 1925, against the Washington Senators; and in 1960, against the New York Yankees. The latter served as a bit of payback for the drubbing the Pirates received from New York in the 1927 Series. The park hosted the All-Star Game in 1944 and 1959, and in 1935, it was the site of Babe Ruth's last three home runs. His last shot cleared the red slate roof in right field, which stood eighty-six feet high. The feat, which has been matched only seventeen times, is believed to be the longest home run in Forbes Field history.

In addition to the Pirates, the Homestead Grays of the Negro League called Forbes Field home. But the park served as much more than a baseball diamond. The NFL's Pittsburgh Steelers played there from 1933 to 1963

Forbes Field's centerfield wall is virtually all that is left standing. Fans gather there every October to celebrate Pittsburgh's victory over the New York Yankees in the 1960 World Series. *Photo by author.*

before moving to Pitt Stadium and, then, to Three Rivers Stadium. The Pitt Panthers also played football there from 1909 to 1924, racking up five undefeated seasons in that period. For a short time, it played host to the Pittsburgh Phantoms professional soccer club, and fight fans flocked to the park to watch scores of professional boxing matches over the years.

The ballpark closed after a double header against the Cubs—who else? The Cubs also were the opponents for the first and last games at old Exposition Park—it was run-down and in need of repair. Bob Prince thought it tragic that the park was closing. He once said that in moving to Three Rivers Stadium, the Pirates "took the players away from the fans." He believed the park could have been saved. But Forbes Field's fate had been sealed twelve years earlier, when the University of Pittsburgh bought the property for $2 million—coincidentally, what Dreyfuss had paid for the land and construction of the ballpark. From then on, it was a matter of time before Forbes Field would become only a memory.

Not entirely, however. Pieces of Forbes Field survive; home plate can be seen—under glass—on the first floor of Pitt's Posvar Hall, and sections of the left-center-field wall are still standing. On October 13 every year, a group of fans gather at the wall to listen to a broadcast of the seventh game of the 1960 World Series, in which second baseman Bill Mazeroski's ninth-inning home run lifted the Bucs to victory. The tradition was started by, and nearly died with, Saul Finkelstein, a Squirrel Hill resident who came to the site on that day in 1985, sat by the flagpole and listened to a rebroadcast of the game by himself. He did this for eight years before anyone joined him, but since then, as many as one thousand fans a year have come to honor the 1960 World Series champions.

14

KDKA RADIO

BROADCAST PIONEER

*O*ne of the accepted facts of Pittsburgh history is that it is the home of the first commercial broadcast station: KDKA. Its first broadcast occurred on November 2, 1920, when the station relayed the results of the Harding-Cox presidential election results. There is a plaque outside of KDKA's headquarters that proclaims that fact.

The truth is quite a bit murkier. First, KDKA—then operating under the call sign 8ZZ—was not the only radio outfit broadcasting the election results that night. Radio stations in St. Louis and Detroit also aired the vote tallies as they were reported. Second, there is plenty of evidence of other radio broadcasts long before 1920. Third, according to the U.S. Department of Commerce, the first broadcasting license was issued in September 1921, to WBZ in Springfield, Massachusetts; KDKA did not receive a license until December of that year. However, since an actual broadcast license issued by the federal government did not exist until 1927, it's hard to tell exactly which stations were allowed to do what in the early days of radio.

Of course, back then, such information was hard to come by, or prove, so the Westinghouse Corporation's statement that KDKA "was the first to give regular broadcasting programs" was not seriously challenged for years. Whatever the reality, it is more than fair to say that KDKA was a pioneer in the radio industry. This is mainly because Harry Davis, vice-president of Westinghouse, realized early on the possibilities of radio to change the business of communications and capitalized on it.

Davis's "light bulb" moment came in September 1920, when he saw a newspaper advertisement for "Amateur Wireless Sets" being sold at Horne's department store in downtown Pittsburgh. This was something Westinghouse could build and sell and profit from—as long as a demand for these sets could be created. This spurred Davis to make sure Westinghouse had a station ready to broadcast by the time election night rolled around.

If Davis was the idea man, Frank Conrad was the facilitator. For several years, Conrad had broadcast from a radiotelegraph station, call sign 8XK, out of his garage in Wilkinsburg, Pennsylvania. Starting with Morse code and eventually transitioning to audio transmissions, Conrad became well known in broadcasting circles. He agreed to work with Westinghouse, which had built an antenna on the roof of a building in Turtle Creek, Pennsylvania. Davis drummed up plenty of publicity surrounding the initial event and then made sure there was a continuing market for radio by putting together a series of regular programs. KDKA began with one hour of programming per day and slowly expanded. But it took a while for

The "tomato can" microphone used to broadcast the 1920 presidential election results from KDKA Radio is now housed in the Smithsonian Institution. *Library of Congress.*

KDKA—actually, radio in general—to catch on. When it did, however, it was an explosion. Within four years, there were six hundred commercial radio stations in the United States.

Although KDKA may not have been the first official radio station, it certainly has set a number of precedents in its first one hundred years. On January 2, 1921, in order to prove that the station could broadcast from a remote location, KDKA aired the first religious service via radio, at Calvary Episcopal Church in Shadyside. Although the Reverend Edwin Van Ettin was so skeptical of this new medium that he decided not to preach that Sunday, deferring to his junior minister, the broadcast was a success, and soon KDKA was broadcasting every Sunday evening from Calvary—with Reverend Van Ettin standing at the pulpit.

This success opened the door to other out-of-the-studio events, particularly in the sports world. On August 5, 1921, KDKA was the first to broadcast a baseball game, when Harold Arlin described the action of the Pirates' matchup against the Philadelphia Phillies at Forbes Field. The next day, Arlin took his equipment to the Allegheny Country Club and broadcast a Davis Cup tennis match between Australia and Great Britain. Later that year, KDKA and two other Westinghouse stations joined forces to air a World Series game for the first time, between the New York Yankees and the New York Giants. Before the year was out, KDKA would also broadcast its first college football game, with Arlin again calling the action between the University of Pittsburgh Panthers and the West Virginia University Mountaineers.

In 1951, the station introduced the listening public to a new kind of radio program, the call-in talk show. Called *Party Line*, it was hosted by Ed and Wendy King. Because the program aired from 9:00 p.m. to midnight, when the airwaves were less cluttered, KDKA's fifty-thousand-watt antenna allowed listeners from all over the country to tune in.

Party Line was different from most of the other talk shows that would follow. First, the conversation could be about anything—except politics. Second, Ed King made the decision early on that phone calls would not be heard on the air. Instead, people would ask questions or voice comments, and Ed or Wendy would paraphrase the call. Ed told many interviewers that the couple wanted the focus to be on the ideas being discussed, rather than on the people calling in. Each evening, the couple would talk about whatever the callers brought up, and they would also read letters from listeners. The show, totally unscripted, was seldom about any of the major issues of the day, and yet *Party Line* was compelling radio, a show that might have lasted much longer than twenty years had Ed King not died of cancer in 1971.

The Kings were but two of the interesting personalities who have lived on KDKA over the years, as the station transitioned from one format to another. "Uncle" Ed Shaughency popularized what would become known as "morning drive time" before moving over to the news desk. He worked for KDKA from 1932 to 1980. Rege Cordic brought comedy to the morning slot in 1954 with a host of strange characters and a penchant for creating fake ads such as the one for "Olde Frothingslosh: the stale pale ale with the foam on the bottom." Art Pallan and Clark Race were two of the more notable DJs in the 1960s, and Jack Bogut came from Salt Lake City to introduce Pittsburghers to the Farkleberry Tart, which was sold at Christmastime to raise money for Children's Hospital. (You can buy Farkleberry cookies these days at the Oakmont Bakery; the treat has an orange flavor, is crammed with dried cranberries and white chocolate chips and is dusted with powdered sugar.)

On April 10, 1992, KDKA switched to a news/talk format. The last song played on the air was Don McLean's "American Pie"—the station's way of announcing that the music, at least on KDKA, had "died."

15

KENNYWOOD PARK

CAROUSELS AND COASTERS

On December 18, 1898, an article appeared in the Sunday edition of the *Pittsburgh Daily Post*. The headline read "New Pleasure Resort Will Be Established." The story confirmed the purchase by the Monongahela Street Railway Company of 160 acres of farmland near the terminus of the railway line in the Monongahela Valley. Plans were sketchy at the time, but the land was to include a picnic area, two observation towers and an open-air auditorium. Because the land had been owned by the Kenny family, the new owners decided to call the picnic grove Kennywood Park.

Designed by George S. Davidson, the railway company's chief engineer, when the park opened the following May, it featured a "dancing pavilion, cottages, a café, tennis courts, baseball grounds and a pretty little chain of lakes," according to the *Pittsburgh Post-Gazette*. There also was a carousel and a casino—not a gambling house but a banquet hall.

Kennywood Park, which celebrated its 120th anniversary in 2018, looks nothing like its original layout. With its famous coasters, dozens of rides and highly regarded Kiddieland, the amusement grounds today make the original park seem quaint and sedate. It surprises some people to learn that when it opened, Kennywood Park upset some people. In an interview with WESA radio in 2015, Brian Butko, who wrote a history of the park, said that Kennywood "offended Victorian mores" because "you could dress more casually and be loud and drink."

That didn't stop people from flocking to the park by the hundreds. Organizations held their outings at the park, and the site soon was offering

Kennywood in the early twentieth century bears little resemblance to the amusement park of today. *Library of Congress*.

something for all ages. In 1901, the Old Mill was built. The following year, the Figure Eight Toboggan—the park's first roller coaster—was added. By 1903, the park had designed uniforms for its employees and added two miniature railroads and a ride called the Steeplechase. The Steeplechase, which lasted for only one year, was an amusement in which customers would race wooden horses down parallel tracks. The ride worked on gravity, but riders had the ability to control the speed of the horses.

Carousels have always been a centerpiece of Kennywood Park. The first, built by Gustav Dentzel, entertained riders from the park's opening until 1913. It was replaced by a merry-go-round designed by the T.M. Harton Company, which, ironically, had opened the rival West View Park on the north side of Pittsburgh in 1906. The Harton carousel was replaced in 1927 with another Dentzel design, this time by William H. Dentzel. Interestingly, that merry-go-round was originally meant to be a ride at the Philadelphia Exposition of 1926. However, it wasn't finished in time for the event. Andrew McSwigan and Fred Henninger, who had leased the park from the now Pittsburgh Railway Company in 1906, were able to purchase it from Dentzel for $25,000, and Philly's loss was Pittsburgh's gain.

But people outside of the Pittsburgh area know Kennywood primarily as a destination for roller-coaster aficionados. And there have been more than a dozen different coasters in the park over its history. From 1902, when the original Figure Eight Toboggan (removed in 1921) was added, until 1950, there was the Dip-the-Dips Scenic Railway (1905–10), the original Racer (1910–26), the Speed-O-Plane (1911–23), the Jack Rabbit (opened 1920), the Pippin (opened 1924, converted to the Thunderbolt in 1968), the Racer (opened 1927), the Brownie (1928–53), the Tickler (1931–52), the Teddy Bear (1935–47) and the Little Dipper (1948–84).

In 1980, the Laser Loop became the first non-wood coaster in the park. It lasted ten years. As of 2019, there were four steel coasters in what was once called "The Roller Coaster Capital of the World": Phantom's Revenge, Sky Rocket, the Steel Curtain and the Exterminator. But patrons still stand in line for the double dip on the Jack Rabbit, the excitement of "competing" against your friends on the Racer and the thrill of the Thunderbolt.

In 1987, Kennywood Park became one of only two amusement parks in the country to be designated a National Historic Landmark. The other designation, also in 1987, went to Rye Playland in Westchester County, New York.

16

MOUNT WASHINGTON

FUEL FOR THE CITY

*T*oday, Mount Washington (which typically includes the Duquesne Heights neighborhood on the western side of the hill) has a major, if not exactly tangible, value to the city as a prime tourist attraction. People come to the Mount mainly for the panoramic view of the city and to ride one of the two inclines for which Pittsburgh is famous. They may spend money in one of the restaurants or shops that rest atop the hillside, but it's hard to quantify what this area means to the city in terms of revenue.

But decades before the city was ever incorporated, Mount Washington had a very real, measurable value to the area, and the neighborhood bore a practical name befitting its contribution to the city: Coal Hill. Beneath the homes of some ten thousand residents and the businesses that support them today is the Pittsburgh seam, a thick ribbon of bituminous coal that actually stretches through southwestern Pennsylvania and into West Virginia. At one time, the Pittsburgh seam was considered to be the most commercially valuable mineral deposit in North America. According to the U.S. Geological Survey, more than one billion tons of coal have been taken from that seam in Allegheny County alone. But the entire seam, stretching through southwestern Pennsylvania into West Virginia, still holds an estimated sixteen billion tons.

Coal was not the only rock that Mount Washington provided the city. Gray sandstone quarried from the Mount was used to build the Allegheny County Courthouse. But it was coal that would help Pittsburgh grow, architecture in the past 200 years" by a survey of architects and historians. In 2005, it was designated a National Historic Landmark.

Because of its view, Mount Washington has been visited by myriad tourists, some of them celebrities. One of the more noteworthy visits was in 1884, when Samuel Clemens, aka Mark Twain, traveled to Pittsburgh to promote *The Adventures of Huckleberry Finn*. Twain possessed a wonderful wit, as demonstrated by his description of his trip to the Mount, printed in the *Pittsburgh Daily Post* on December 31, 1884:

> *With the moon soft and mellow floating in the heavens, we sauntered about the mount, and looked down on the lake of fire and flame. It looked like a miniature hell with the lid off. It was a vision. A wonderful vision. It tended to frighten. The view is not as deliciously beautiful as one would suppose. If one can be calm and resolute he can look upon the picture and still live. Otherwise, your city is a beauty.*

POINT STATE PARK

THE GOLDEN TRIANGLE'S GREEN

*T*he confluence of the Allegheny, Monongahela and Ohio Rivers has been the site of everything from a military installation to an exposition center to a blighted industrial and residential area. But when the renaissance of downtown Pittsburgh occurred in the middle of the twentieth century, the "Point" became an important element of the city's rebirth. Today, with its fountain, footbridge, historical sites and scores of native plants, the thirty-six acres at the tip of the Golden Triangle have become a local treasure, frequented by residents and tourists and host to a variety of cultural and entertainment events.

Point State Park was officially dedicated in 1974 and became a National Historic Landmark the following year. But its genesis came in the 1940s, when Mayor David L. Lawrence decided it was long past time for the city to clean up its act. The city had been referred to in several pejorative ways over the years—"The Smoky City" and "Hell with the lid off," for example—and the soot and ash from numerous steel mills and other coal-fired manufacturing plants had caused numerous health problems and made Pittsburgh a less than desirable place to live. Lawrence wanted to change that, and with several prominent businessmen and the support of the Allegheny Conference on Community Development, he began to change the look and feel of the city.

One of those efforts was to clean up the Point. Prior to the 1850s, the Point was a residential and commercial area, with the Monongahela Wharf serving as the departure point for businesspeople to ship their goods. But once the Pennsylvania Railroad arrived in Pittsburgh, the city's economic structure changed. Commercial enterprises moved more to the interior of the city, and the Point became the site of industrial plants, warehouses and railroad yards as Pittsburgh became best known for the production of iron, steel, glass, aluminum and more.

Over time, the area fell into disrepair. Time after time, however, discussions about renovating the area went unheeded. Even Frederick Law Olmsted Jr., architect of the National Mall and Jefferson Memorial in Washington, D.C., couldn't sway city officials. It would take the aftereffects of the Great Depression and the onset of World War II before the city would decide to take action.

Even then, community leaders were divided as to what the land should become. Many wanted a park, while others, such as Edgar Kaufmann, owner of Kaufmann's Department Store, conceived of a more urban use. Kaufmann even brought in architect Frank Lloyd Wright to develop plans for a multiuse civic center. Elected officials rejected Wright's design as being too expensive, and ultimately, the land was purchased from its various owners for the park that stands there today. Behind the park, land was condemned, and Gateway Center grew in its place.

Architects Ralph Griswold and Charles Stotz were hired to design the park. It would take nearly thirty years for the construction to be completed. For example, the Point and Manchester Bridges were connected to the Point, and they would not be demolished until 1970. Only then could workers construct the six-thousand-gallon-per-minute fountain that stands there today. Meanwhile, the Fort Pitt and Fort Duquesne Bridges were being built alongside the older spans. Once those two bridges were connected, the architects' design of a fifty-foot-wide walkway, running underneath the bridges' overpass and spanning a reflective pool, could be realized. Finally, the city could truly claim it was developing a Golden Triangle.

In the process of designing the park, only one building was left standing: the Fort Pitt Blockhouse. The Blockhouse, possibly the oldest structure still in existence in western Pennsylvania, had been deeded to the Daughters of the American Revolution (DAR) in 1894 by Mary Schenley, who owned the property on which the building stood. Over the years, suggestions had been made about relocating the building, but officials wisely decided to leave it in proximity to the remains of Fort Pitt itself. When Point State Park was developed, three of the fort's five bastions were reconstructed. One of those, the Monongahela Bastion, is where the Fort Pitt Museum was built in 1969, giving the park historical, cultural and recreational significance.

The Point was once a congested industrial and residential section of Pittsburgh's downtown. *Library of Congress.*

Fort Pitt, of course, is not the only military installation to have stood at the Point. In fact, it is merely the longest standing of four forts to have graced the area. To the earliest settlers to the region, the Point was seen as a vital site from which to defend their claims. In the mid-1750s, both the British and the French sought to control the area. The French laid claim to the Point, arguing that because the Ohio River was part of the Mississippi River basin—which the French controlled—they were legally entitled to it. But the British, in the form of the Virginia colony, also claimed the land; in 1754, they asked the French to leave. When the French refused, a small Virginia garrison headed to the Point and began building Fort Prince George. Two months into construction, the fort was overwhelmed by French forces, and the Virginians surrendered.

The French built Fort Du Quesne, the outline of which today is marked in granite in the park. They held the area for four years during the French and Indian War, but in 1758, they fled before an advancing army of British soldiers, burning the fort to the ground as they left. The British built Fort Mercer as a temporary structure, and the following year, they constructed

The Fort Pitt Blockhouse, donated to the Daughters of the American Revolution by Mary Schenley in 1896, keeps history alive at Point State Park. *Library of Congress.*

Fort Pitt. This fort remained in use off and on for more than thirty years until it was officially abandoned in 1792. The fort originally was decommissioned in 1772 and sold to a group of private citizens. But with the start of the Revolutionary War, the Continental army took back control of the fort, which served as its western headquarters.

When Fort Lafayette was built in 1792, nearer to the Strip District, Fort Pitt was dismantled and its building materials sold to local residents, who used them to help construct their own homes. Only the Blockhouse, which in the 1780s had been remade into a residence, remained. Its first owner was Major Isaac Craig, and a number of people lived there until 1802, when James O'Hara purchased the land. When he died, his granddaughter assumed ownership until she turned the blockhouse over to the DAR. The blockhouse was designated a National Historic Landmark in 1960.

At the start of the new millennium, a master plan was created to renew the park, which was beginning to show its age. Beginning in 2006, at a cost of $25 million, the Point State Park Capital Renovation Project refurbished the area, including major upgrades to the fountain, which was closed for four years, from 2009 to 2013.

THE CIVIC ARENA

THE "IGLOO"

*I*f there were a vote to determine the most iconic building in Pittsburgh's history, odds are the winner would be the Civic Arena. Known affectionately by locals as the "Igloo," the arena stood for nearly fifty years as the site of sporting events, concerts, musical plays, car and boat shows, political rallies and more. From the Ice Capades Show on September 19, 1961, to a performance by James Taylor and Carole King on June 26, 2010, this architectural and engineering marvel entertained millions of residents and tourists.

Although the arena brought international recognition to a city being reborn in the 1950s and '60s, the planning and construction of the Civic Arena was fraught with controversy, and the circumstances of its coming into being have left a stain on the city's history that has yet to be cleansed. But that doesn't diminish what the building itself has meant to Pittsburgh.

The story began in 1946, when the organization known as the Civic Light Opera (CLO) was formed. The CLO was created to showcase the performing arts, particularly Broadway musicals. The CLO's first season took place at Pitt Stadium, atop "Cardiac Hill" on the campus of the University of Pittsburgh. Of course, outdoor theater is subject to the vagaries of the weather, and more than a few performances that season were canceled due to rain.

City councilman Abe Wolk, who had convinced department-store magnate Edgar Kaufmann to underwrite the CLO, came back to Kaufmann with an idea of building a new home for the group. Wolk suggested that the venue have a retractable roof so that outdoor theater could be realized without the threat of costly postponements. Kaufmann ran with the idea, commissioning Frank Lloyd Wright to design it.

Wright's vision was grand: a complex thirteen levels high, with an amphitheater, three additional performance spaces, a sports facility and an exhibition hall. Wright's design was to be built on the most stunning space possible: the Point, where Pittsburgh's Allegheny and Monongahela Rivers meet to form the Ohio River. Kaufmann went to the Allegheny Conference on Community Development for approval and funding, but the design was rejected as too costly.

Unbowed, Kaufmann scaled back the plans to include just an amphitheater. He hired architects James Mitchell and Dahlen Ritchey, who came up with a design that featured a fabric roof attached to a cantilevered arm. The city approved the design, but by this time, in the early 1950s, the city had decided to develop the Point as a park. So, a new site was chosen: the lower Hill District, 105 acres of which the Urban Redevelopment Authority had slated for demolition.

At about the same time, Mayor David L. Lawrence had decided that the Duquesne Gardens, the five-thousand-seat sports arena that was home to the Pittsburgh Hornets of the American Hockey League, needed to be replaced. He suggested combining the CLO venture with a sports arena as a multipurpose facility. Mitchell and Richey went back to the drawing board and came back with a plan that was, in its own way, as ambitious as Frank Lloyd Wright's original plan for the Point. In addition to an auditorium with a retractable steel dome, the duo designed an arts complex that would include a concert hall, a theater, an art museum and exhibition space, along with upscale apartments and office buildings.

In September 1955, after securing more than $17 million in grants and loans from the federal government, city council approved plans for the arena, a concert hall, a hotel and what would become the Washington Plaza Apartments. Construction on the auditorium began in 1958, and in September 1961, the Civic Arena was dedicated. (Its given name was Civic Auditorium, but that reportedly was changed after some signmakers decided it was easier to print "Civic Arena" on the signs.)

Covering 170,000 square feet, the auditorium was an impressive structure that appeared to be mostly roof. Composed of eight steel panels, each weighing three hundred tons, the roof was supported by a single cantilevered arm, 260 feet long, on the outside of the roof. The design made it possible for patrons to have an unobstructed view of the stage,

The shape of the Civic Arena led to its being affectionately called the "Igloo" by fans and is one of the reasons the city's pro hockey team is known as the Penguins. *Wikimedia Commons*.

court or rink. Six of the roof's panels were connected to hydraulic jacks and could be retracted fully within two minutes. With bated breath, the arena crew opened the roof on the afternoon of the Civic Arena's first scheduled event, the Ice Capades. But it took the men only twenty-two minutes to realize that the outside temperature—seventy-four degrees that afternoon—would likely turn the rink ice to mush before the show even began. So, they quickly closed it. The roof's "opening" party didn't occur until ten months later, on July 4, 1962, for a performance by the CLO featuring Carol Burnett.

The roof was an engineering feat that for several years was unique. Unfortunately, it never lived up to the hype. It is a trifle ironic that the original occupant of the arena, the Civic Light Opera, suffered most from the challenges the roof created. In addition to the roof having to remain closed during inclement weather, it also couldn't be opened if it were too windy, as the breeze would swirl through the auditorium and play havoc with scenery. Nor could it be opened for rock concerts, because the lighting for such events was hung from the roof. Also, when the roof was open, acoustics were severely compromised. And finally, the design of the domed roof made it difficult for the CLO to hang appropriate lighting or scenery, and the installation of permanent sets of the type found in most theaters was impossible in the arena. After a few frustrating years as a tenant, in

1969, the CLO gave up on the arena. In 1971, it relocated to Heinz Hall. Its last Civic Arena show was the musical *How Now, Dow Jones* on July 26, 1969. Musical theater would return to the arena one last time, in July 1971, when *Jesus Christ Superstar* was performed, three months before the show opened on Broadway.

Even after the departure of the CLO, the operating costs of the dome—including frequent repairs to its hydraulics—caused personnel to be judicious in their decisions on when to retract the dome. The official end of dome openings came in 1995, when the roof became the support for the huge Jumbotron scoreboard and video monitor.

But retractable roof or no, the Civic Arena became famous for two contrasting types of events: sports and musical concerts. The first of the latter events was October 19, 1961, when Judy Garland sang for a sellout crowd of more than twelve thousand fans. The crowd loved her, and she loved them back, coming out for six encores. The following night, the La Rells became the first Pittsburgh group to grace the arena stage, as part of the first Rock and Roll Show, hosted by DJ Clark Race. The show included Fats Domino, Brenda Lee and others. As a concert venue, the Civic Arena hosted everyone from the Beatles and the Rolling Stones to Frank Sinatra, Elvis Presley and Garth Brooks. Dozens of acts came to the arena every year; in 1976, *Billboard* magazine named it the ninth-best concert venue in the United States.

As for sports, in addition to the Hornets and, later, the Penguins hockey teams, the arena was at one time or another home to the Pittsburgh Pipers and Condors of the American Basketball Association, the Triangles of World Team Tennis, the Spirit of the Major Indoor Soccer League, the Stingers of the Continental Indoor Soccer League and the Duquesne Dukes NCAA basketball team. The arena also was the site of boxing matches, figure skating championships, wrestling extravaganzas, high school basketball games and even roller derby matchups featuring the New York Chiefs.

But as the new millennium dawned, the Igloo began to show its age, and by 2005, the Penguins were clamoring for a new arena. Owner Mario Lemieux threatened to move the team, possibly to Kansas City, unless a new home was built for the team. This was the death knell for the Civic Arena. As part of the agreement between the city and the Penguins, the old arena could not be used for any type of event that would compete with the new site. All that was left now was to determine whether the arena would remain standing as a preserved historic structure. Several governmental bodies, including Pittsburgh City Council, voted against historical status, and on September 26, 2011, the destruction of the arena began. By the end of March 2012, the Civic Arena was no more.

The arena had brought international distinction to Pittsburgh, not only as an architectural gem but also as a venue for so many types of events. But there was a steep price to pay. The people of the Hill District, who thought the arena and other planned cultural venues would revitalize a worn-down neighborhood, saw only destruction. Promised housing for the displaced never materialized, and the area immediately north of the arena never recovered. Not only that, but the demolition of the lower Hill also included several well-known jazz clubs. A large chunk of musical history was razed, and Pittsburgh lost its status as a premier city for jazz. (For more on this, see the chapters "David L. Lawrence" and "Jazz.")

19

THE STRIP DISTRICT

A CYCLE OF REBIRTH

*I*t may be a cliché to refer to a person or a place as having nine lives, but the Strip District certainly has had its share of incarnations— and even a near-death experience. It also has been known by several different names: Shannopin's Town, Northern Liberties, Bayardstown, Denny's Bottoms and the Fifth Ward, for example. How the Strip District came to be known by its current name is unclear, but most likely it comes from the fact that the land is literally a half-mile strip three blocks wide and twenty-two blocks long. It runs east–west from Eleventh Street to Thirty-Third Street, with three major thoroughfares: Smallman Street, Liberty Avenue and Penn Avenue.

One thing the Strip has always been, however, is an economic focal point for the city. Its proximity to the Allegheny River made it an ideal site to locate manufacturing plants, and several famous companies got their start in this neighborhood. Westinghouse Air Brake, Fort Pitt Foundry, the Pittsburgh Reduction Company (which later became ALCOA) and U.S. Steel all began their lives in the Strip. Iron mills, glass factories and even a cork factory were located here in the nineteenth century.

A decision by the Pennsylvania Railroad at the turn of the last century paved the way for a kind of rebirth of the Strip, from an industrial center to a wholesalers' market. Prior to 1906, the railroad ran a train all the way down Liberty Avenue to the 600 block of Liberty downtown. Produce and other food goods were delivered to the terminus, and wholesalers would pick up their goods and store them in nearby warehouses. But when the

Looking east up Smallman Street in the Strip District, facing St. Stanislaus Kostka Church. *Wikimedia Commons.*

railroad decided to remove those tracks, wholesalers began to relocate closer to the Pennsylvania Railroad yards—which happened to be in the Strip District. Industries began to move out of the Strip to other, more expansive locations along the rivers, and wholesalers and other food manufacturers took their place. The new hub of the Strip became the produce station, located at Twenty-First Street, and warehouses began to spring up in either direction—the larger ones locating on Smallman Street and smaller ones dotting Penn and Liberty Avenues. Other food-related companies also opened: Pennsylvania Macaroni Company and H.J. Heinz, for example.

A series of unfortunate events, all out of the control of the companies located there, threatened to destroy the Strip as an economic force. The first was the Great Depression, which of course hit the businesses hard. If that weren't enough, on March 17, 1936, a flood of staggering proportions inundated much of downtown, including the Strip. The floodwaters peaked at forty-six feet—twenty-one feet above flood stage. The city had never seen a flood this devastating—and likely never will again; the following year, work began on a number of flood control systems on the Allegheny and Monongahela Rivers.

Companies slowly dug themselves out of this financial hole, only to be socked yet again when World War II broke out with its food rationing and price freezes. Although the postwar years brought relief for many wholesalers, the Strip District would never be the same. Long-haul trucks replaced railroads as the major delivery mode, making the Strip less important. The 1950s also saw the growth of chain supermarkets, which not only put a number of small "mom-and-pop" stores out of business but also threatened the wholesale industry because these large chains were more likely to cut out the middleman in their purchasing strategies. According to the website Strip District Neighbors, in the 1950s there were seventy-one wholesale produce dealers in the Strip. Twenty years later, that number was down to about twenty-four, but many of these companies decided to reinvent themselves by opening retail outlets.

So, too, did the Strip District reinvent itself. Just as it was known in the nineteenth century for its ethnic mix of residents and businesspeople, the Strip once again drew in immigrants. Joining the Italians, Greeks, Poles and Slavs were Asian, Middle Eastern, African, Caribbean and other ethnic groups opening stores and restaurants, bars and nightclubs. High-end eateries such as Lidia's, Eleven, Kaya, Crystal and Cioppino's Restaurant and Cigar Bar are today's popular nightspots. The neighborhood now draws in another kind of nightlife: instead of produce buyers and truckers frequenting places such as Primanti's, theatergoers and club hoppers traverse the streets of the Strip.

The transformation is ongoing. In 2016, McCaffery Interests, a Chicago company, announced plans to renovate the Produce Terminal and 1600 Smallman Street, directly across the street, and populate it with shops, restaurants, offices and even apartments. The project is projected to cost $100 million.

20

U.S. STEEL, ALCOA AND PPG

THEIR BUILDINGS' LEGACIES

Considered individually, the Alcoa Building, U.S. Steel Tower and PPG Place could each be seen by Pittsburghers as iconic because of their height and/or visibility in the downtown area. However, another way to look at these three skyscrapers is as a group, representative of the three industries that drove the city's economy for more than a century. Not only were they built by companies that dominated manufacturing here, but they were also constructed using as their primary component the very materials their owners produced.

The oldest of the three is the Alcoa Building, which is now known as the Regional Enterprise Tower. Built in 1953, the thirty-story structure is 410 feet tall. It has never been the tallest of Pittsburgh's skyscrapers—it ranks fifteenth in that category today—but as a model of efficiency and economy in construction there are few buildings in the world that can match it.

The structure, designed to demonstrate the many possible uses of aluminum, was the first of its kind in the world. The building's façade is constructed of prefabricated aluminum sheets, a mere one-eighth of an inch thick, attached to a steel frame. Because of aluminum's light weight, the building's skeleton required only 6,500 tons of steel. By comparison, its neighbor, the Gulf Building, needed twice as much steel, and it was only seven stories taller. The prefab sheets even included the windows, made of fifty-by-fifty-five-inch, double-paned plate glass that could rotate 360 degrees, making them easier to clean. In addition, the windows were sealed using inflatable neoprene to make climate control easier.

Another interesting facet of the building is a radiant heating and cooling system built into the ceiling of each story. It was lightweight, efficient and space-saving. Eliminating the usual heaters and air conditioners that were typically built into walls gave Alcoa an additional fifteen thousand square feet of office space—the equivalent of one and a half floors. Practically everything in the building gives testimony to what aluminum can do. Pipes, HVAC ducts, even most of the furniture, were made with aluminum.

Alcoa moved from its headquarters to a new building on the North Side of the city in 2001, when executives decided the company needed more open floor space. The building now has a mix of government offices and private apartments. But it still stands as a lightweight structure that was a heavyweight in innovation.

The U.S. Steel Tower, opened in 1971, also featured a new product. The skyscraper, still the tallest building in Pittsburgh, is distinctive with its steel columns on the outside—forty-four thousand metric tons of Cor-Ten steel. Cor-Ten was made to eliminate a need endemic to steel structures, that of rust-prevention maintenance. Cor-Ten steel "paints" itself by forming a brownish exterior rust that actually prevents deeper oxidation, forgoing the need for periodic painting and rust-proofing. The columns themselves are filled with a mixture of water, antifreeze and rust inhibitor, making them fireproof. The tower also was designed with redundant water, electrical, heating and cooling systems, which make the building virtually immune to emergencies such as loss of power.

The building, which now features the initials "UPMC" to signify the building's largest tenant—University of Pittsburgh Medical Center—is notable for a couple of other reasons. First, its triangular shape is uniform from top to bottom, meaning that the roof is the same square footage as every other floor, one acre. This makes it the largest roof of any building of its size. In its early years, the roof served as a heliport, but since then several ideas to create another use for the space have gone unexplored. The most recent known concept, in 2013, was a two-story glass atrium. Until 2001, of course, residents and visitors who wanted to partake of the view could dine at the Top of the Triangle, a Stouffer's restaurant. But when that restaurant closed, the space was converted to offices.

PPG Place, opened in 1983 and officially dedicated in April 1984, is the most recent of the three structures. But the company that built it, PPG Industries, is actually the oldest of the three companies. It was founded in 1883 as Pittsburgh Plate Glass by John Baptiste Ford and John Pitcairn Jr. (ALCOA was founded as Pittsburgh Reduction Company in 1888, and U.S.

The former headquarters of Alcoa is a monument to the many uses of aluminum.
Wikimedia Commons.

Steel was incorporated in 1901.) Originally headquartered in Creighton, Pennsylvania, the company was the first to commercially produce plate glass. The company's offices moved to Pittsburgh in 1895 and were located on Fourth Avenue about a block or so from where its headquarters is now.

PPG Place, which includes six buildings and a plaza covering five and a half acres, may not be the tallest skyscraper in the city, but it is arguably the most impressive. It was constructed using one million square feet of PPG

The PPG complex in downtown Pittsburgh showcases the company's first and major product: glass. *Wikimedia Commons*.

Solarban 550 Twindow—nearly 20,000 pieces of it—and features 231 glass spires, the tallest being eighty-two feet. Solarban is an energy-efficient glass, reflecting heat in the summer and storing it in the winter. The twenty-one elevators in the main, forty-story tower are composed of clear glass panels, as well as fractured glass. Architecture critic Charles L. Rosenblum called the complex "Gothic Revival in style, reimagined in glass." Another critic referred to it as "one of the most ambitious, sensitive and public-spirited urban developments since Rockefeller Center."

In 1999, PPG sold the complex to the Hillman Company, which set about to make the area more inviting to the public. In 2001, the company installed in the plaza an ice-skating rink, which is typically open from November to March. During the holiday season, the center of the rink is decorated with a sixty-five-foot-tall Christmas tree, which covers the red granite obelisk that dominates the plaza the rest of the year. In the warmer months, the rink is dismantled and the plaza's obelisk is surrounded by a water fountain with 140 water jets and illuminated by 280 underground lights.

21

WQED-TV

A PUBLIC FIRST

*J*ust as it had with KDKA radio in 1920, Pittsburgh once again became a broadcasting pioneer on April 1, 1954, when WQED-TV went on the air for the first time. WQED was not the first public broadcasting station in the country; what set it apart from outlets such as WGBH in Boston was its funding source. WQED was the first National Education Television (the predecessor of PBS) station in the country not bankrolled by a university. Virtually all of its operating capital came from private sources: corporations and private citizens giving money and donations in kind.

An interesting cast of characters helped give birth to WQED and helped fuel its early success. Mayor David L. Lawrence got the ball rolling in 1951, when he petitioned the Federal Communications Commission to grant a license for an educational station. The late 1940s and early 1950s was a wild time at the FCC, as dozens of individuals and companies wanted to get in on this new form of media. The FCC had so many applications on file that it had to put a freeze on new applications.

However, because Mayor Lawrence was a persuasive and connected individual—he counted then-president Harry Truman among his friends— the FCC granted Pittsburgh a license, provided Lawrence was able to generate enough money to get—and keep—the station running.

He turned to Leland Hazard, an attorney for Pittsburgh Plate Glass and the vice-president and cultural chair of the Allegheny Conference on Community Development, to bring this dream to life. Hazard used his influence to convince the conference to sponsor the station in principle. That, as well as a grant from the Ford Foundation, was the first step. Other funding came from various trusts and foundations, but raising money was hard. Hazard once noted that "corporations would not look at it; 'educational television, what's that?'" But he credited three local women with helping to beat the drum for the station: Leonore Elkus, Carolyn Patterson and Dorothy Daniel.

Of the three, Dorothy Daniel would lead the charge. A writer who had experience with radio and TV work in Chicago before moving to Pittsburgh, she was appointed the station's general manager. Her funding efforts were about as grassroots as you could imagine. She visited women's clubs, PTAs, school administrators—anyone who would listen—trying to raise money. Her campaign was simple: donate $2 to help the city provide educational programming. She and her team managed to raise $120,000 this way, and on April 1, 1954, WQED went on the air with a twenty-hour-per-week schedule.

The station was using a mansion at Fifth and Bellefield Avenues that had been donated by the University of Pittsburgh (the School of Music stands there today) and a broadcast tower given to it by the Westinghouse Corporation, which a year later would bring KDKA-TV into being. Its call letters, chosen by Daniel, reflected the station's mission: the QED represents the Latin phrase *quod erat demonstrandum*; "that which was to be shown."

Daniel proved to be a keen judge of talent, and she got children's programming off the ground in an interesting way. She took her secretary, Josephine Vicari, and made her WQED's first TV personality. Vicari was active in local theater as a writer, actor and director, and Daniel thought those talents would serve the station well. Daniel changed Vicari's name to Josie Carey, and she and a young writer and producer named Fred Rogers were given free rein to create *The Children's Corner*. (Daniel had hired Rogers as WQED's program director.) The program went on the air that first day with Carey as the on-air talent and Rogers as the puppeteer behind the scenes, and the show quickly became a hit with children.

WQED's future as a world-famous source of children's programming was foreshadowed that very first week, when the puppet Daniel Striped Tiger popped out from the cuckoo clock that was part of *The Children's Corner* set. According to Deborah Acklin, WQED's CEO in 2018, "On March 31, Mrs. Daniel threw a cocktail party for everyone involved with the station and gave out party favors. She gave Fred Rogers a tiger puppet. One day they needed to fill time on *The Children's Corner*, so Fred had the stage crew cut out a hole in the flat behind Josie. Out popped the tiger. Fred had named the puppet

The current headquarters of WQED-TV. *Wikimedia Commons*.

Daniel Striped Tiger in honor of Mrs. Daniel. You could see Mister Rogers' Neighborhood taking shape early on at *The Children's Corner*."

The Children's Corner aired for seven years, until Carey left WQED to develop children's programming for KDKA. In 1955, the program won a Sylvania Award—the Emmy of its day—for excellence in children's television.

Over the years, the station became known for a number of innovative programs. In 1955, it was the first TV station to air classes for elementary schools, when Pittsburgh began the Metropolitan School Service. In 1968, it launched what undeniably is its most famous export, *Mister Rogers' Neighborhood*. But WQED had its hand in quite a few other programs. It produced the National Geographic specials for fifteen years. In cooperation with WGBH Boston, it developed *Where in the World Is Carmen Sandiego?* and *Where in Time Is Carmen Sandiego? Black Horizons*, first broadcast in 1968, still airs, making it the longest-running program in the country dedicated to African American issues.

Today, as the cliché goes, WQED is not your parents' public broadcasting station. Education is still its mission, but TV is no longer its only teaching vehicle, or even the primary one.

"We are still very active in educational services but most of that is not on radio or television," said Acklin. "It's not visible to the eye but is a very strong part of our mission. In 1954, you worked with the schools because that's all there was. But the philosophy of education has changed and grown and morphed into any place, anything, any experience, any environment as a place for learning. We do a lot of informal education: libraries, community centers, etc. Every spring we do an education summit, where we bring all our partners together to talk about what we're doing and see what they need."

That doesn't mean TV has lost value. WQED still creates programming that it distributes to PBS stations around the country, such as *IQ, Smart Parents*, which helps parents understand and navigate the electronic age with their children. Rick Sebak—who, incidentally, was an intern for Josie Carey in the 1980s when she produced a children's show for a South Carolina TV station—has become a local celebrity for his series of programs detailing Pittsburgh history. The station also has produced shows aimed at some of the most important topics of the day, including opioids, veterans' issues and mental health.

"What we grew up with was public broadcasting," said Acklin. "That has morphed into public media. We grew up with one QED, and it was on a box in the corner. Now we program five different multi-task digital channels on TV. We have a YouTube channel, a Facebook channel, and have all kinds of content on our website. We have a feature for mobile devices called Passbook. It's basically on-demand programming. We need to be where people are and be relevant in their lives."

PART III

Things

22

BRIDGES

PITTSBURGH'S ESSENTIAL STRUCTURES

*B*efore we delve into the history and trivia surrounding Pittsburgh's vast array of bridges, let's set the record straight regarding a bit of boasting Pittsburghers like to do. Pittsburgh has a lot of bridges—446 within the city limits and roughly 2,000 in Allegheny County—but it does not have the most bridges in the world.

True, the city is home to more bridges than Venice, Italy, which has 409. But it pales in comparison to Hamburg, Germany (2,300), and Amsterdam, Netherlands (1,291). It even has fewer bridges than New York City (788), although, to be fair, New York's five boroughs cover a lot more geography than Pittsburgh. We can debate what is counted as a bridge in some of these cities—do footbridges count?—but which town has bragging rights doesn't really matter. Pittsburgh is known for its bridges, and let's leave it at that.

It stands to reason that when your city is founded at the confluence of three rivers, bridges are going to be a defining element. But it took a while for the young city, founded in 1758, to construct its first official bridge—sixty years, to be exact. Before then, ferries were used to carry people from the banks of the Allegheny and Monongahela Rivers to the city.

In 1818, the Monongahela Bridge was built, on roughly the same site as the current Smithfield Street Bridge. The following year, the Allegheny River Bridge was built, crossing the Allegheny River at what would one day become Sixth Street. Both spans were covered wood bridges. In addition, the Allegheny Bridge was a toll bridge. The builder, the Allegheny Bridge

Company, charged people two cents each to cross between Pittsburgh and what was then the city of Allegheny.

Over the years, as building materials evolved and the city grew in both size and population, more and sturdier bridges were constructed to handle increasing traffic—first from people, horses and carts, then from streetcars, buses, cars and trucks. As a result, many of Pittsburgh's current spans are third- or fourth-generation structures.

For instance, the Smithfield Street Bridge is the third bridge to occupy that crossing. The original, the Monongahela Bridge, was destroyed by fire in 1845. The following year, an engineer named John Roebling was hired to design a new bridge. Roebling, a native of Prussia who immigrated to the United States in 1831, had developed a technique for weaving strands of wire into a kind of rope. He used this technique in 1845 to reconstruct the Allegheny Aqueduct, which had been damaged by an ice jam the previous winter. He replicated this for the first Smithfield Street Bridge the following year. That bridge would stand until 1881, when heavier traffic created the need for a replacement.

The present Smithfield Street Bridge is the third span to occupy that site over the Monongahela River. *Library of Congress.*

The new bridge was designed by a man who saw into the future. Gustav Lindenthal created a steel structure that was designed to be upgraded as conditions dictated. The bridge, which opened in 1883, is still in use today, making it the oldest steel bridge in the United States. In that time, it has been renovated or expanded on four separate occasions. In 1974, the bridge was declared a historic landmark, and it survived a bid by the city to close it in the 1990s.

Roebling himself would eventually relocate to Brooklyn, New York, where he would gain lasting fame for his design of the Brooklyn Bridge. But before that, he would build one more span in Pittsburgh, the St. Clair Street Bridge. Constructed in 1857, the iron suspension bridge replaced the Allegheny River Bridge. The St. Clair Bridge would last until 1892, and its successor stood until 1928, when the present Sixth Street Bridge was built.

Of course, the Sixth Street Bridge today is known as the Roberto Clemente Bridge, in honor of one of the greatest and most beloved Pittsburgh Pirates baseball players. Next to it sits the Seventh Street Bridge, opened in 1926, which is also called the Andy Warhol Bridge, commemorating the iconic pop artist. Next to that is the Ninth Street Bridge, now named the Rachel Carson Bridge, after the famed local environmental activist and author of the book *Silent Spring.* It also opened in 1926.

This trio of bridges is known as The Three Sisters, and they share more than an Aztec gold paint job. They share the same self-anchored suspension design, making them the only three identical, side-by-side bridges in the United States.

But the most famous—or should we say infamous?—bridge in Pittsburgh is the Fort Duquesne Bridge. Connecting downtown Pittsburgh at the Point with the near North Side, the Fort Duquesne Bridge itself was completed in 1963. There was a slight problem, however. The city had yet to acquire the rights-of-way to build the ramps that would connect it with the roads on the North Side.

The bridge became a monument to political inefficiency, since red tape and disagreements among various government entities delayed the acquisitions of the necessary real estate for several years. The bridge became known as the "Bridge to Nowhere." It seemed as though it would take a tragedy to get everyone together to resolve the situation. As it turned out, that nearly happened.

In December 1964, a car driven by a twenty-one-year-old student from the University of Pittsburgh drove off the end of the bridge, flying ninety feet in the air before landing at the edge of the Allegheny (or is it the Ohio?)

The "Three Sisters," identical bridges that span the Allegheny River at Sixth, Seventh and Ninth Streets. *Wikimedia Commons.*

River, on its roof. Why? We will never know. Although the driver was unhurt, he claimed not to remember his epic flight, saying only that he may have mistaken the bridge ramp as the entrance to the Parkway East. (Apparently, the barricades he drove through at the south end of the bridge weren't enough of a clue.)

That spurred the city into action—to build stronger barricades. However, shortly after the incident, it was announced that plans were finally underway to finish the highway and build the ramps that would make the bridge whole. The work was supposed to take "two to three years," according to a report in the *Pittsburgh Post-Gazette*. In fact, it took nearly five years to complete, and the bridge opened in 1969.

Circling back to the rest of the 446 bridges within the city itself, there is a span still counted in that total, even though it technically no longer exists. It is the Bellefield Bridge, a stone arch bridge constructed in 1898 to cross over St. Pierre's Ravine, near where the main branch of the Carnegie Library of Pittsburgh stands. But the bridge suffered an ignoble fate, one that admittedly doesn't happen to bridges very often. It was buried.

Shortly after the turn of the last century, city officials decided they wanted to flatten the downtown area. So, they began excavating the area around Grant Street. Lowering the ground by as much as thirty feet in some spots leaves a lot of debris, and it had to go somewhere. It was hauled to St. Pierre's Ravine, and by 1915, the entire ravine had been filled in. Officials decided it would be too expensive to demolish the Bellefield Bridge, so they just left it there to be buried.

Today, the bridge "supports" Schenley Plaza and the Henry Clay Frick Fine Arts Building at the University of Pittsburgh. This is ironic, in a way, because, back in the day, some architects considered the Bellefield Bridge to be a piece of fine art, one of the most beautiful of its kind in the country.

23

GULF TOWER

PITTSBURGH'S WEATHER BEACON

For thirty-eight years, the Gulf Tower on Grant Street in downtown Pittsburgh was not only the tallest building in the city, it was also the tallest building in the state. It gave up the title in 1970, when the U.S. Steel Tower was constructed, literally across the street.

But for most Pittsburghers, the Gulf building is most known not for its height but for its function as the city's unofficial weather beacon. The otherwise Art Deco structure, rising 582 feet in the sky and containing forty-four floors, is topped with a step pyramid that resembles the Mausoleum at Halicarnassus, one of the Seven Wonders of the Ancient World.

The building's first manager, Edward H. Heath, is credited with coming up with the idea to illuminate the six levels of the roof with neon lights in Gulf Oil's colors: blue and orange. The lights, he determined, could be used to "forecast" the weather. Heath worked out a simple setup: steady blue lights would indicate that the weather would be colder but fair; flashing blue meant colder temperatures and precipitation on the horizon. Conversely, steady orange meant warmer, fair weather; flashing orange signaled warmer temperatures but rain in the offing. At the time, the building dwarfed practically every other building in town—the Grant Building, the next tallest, was nearly one hundred feet shorter—so the roof could be seen at night for miles. The lights were adjusted every twelve hours by a security guard in the lobby.

The weather beacon is not unique to Pittsburgh, but the Gulf building's may be the oldest one still in existence. Other examples can be found atop

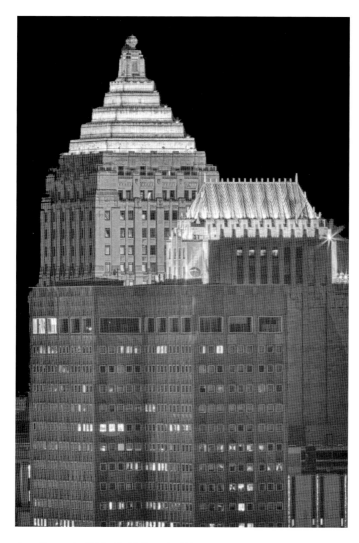

The top of the Gulf Tower has long served as a weather beacon for the city's residents. *Wikimedia Commons*.

the Canada Life Building in Toronto, the Berkeley Building in Boston, the South Tower of One Rincon Hill in San Francisco and the Beyazit Tower in Istanbul. (Before the Beyazit Tower—built in 1828—began forecasting the weather in 2010, it was a fire watch tower.) And in Osaka, Japan, people can learn about the coming weather by viewing the Tempozan Ferris Wheel, the colored lights of which serve that purpose.

The top of the Gulf building burned brightly for more than four decades, until it became a victim of the energy crisis in the late 1970s. (A 2012 article in the *Post-Gazette* compared the cost of lighting the tower back then to providing power for twenty-eight houses.) From then until 2012, only the light at the very top of the roof was used. That year, KDKA-TV partnered with Rugby Realty, the building's current owner, to rewire the pyramid with 185 four-foot-long LED lights.

The new lighting is more complex than its predecessor. But it doesn't predict the weather. Instead, it relays current weather conditions. The top three floors indicate the temperature—from dark blue (below zero degrees Fahrenheit) all the way to bright red (eighty degrees and higher). The level below those marks precipitation, with bluish purple meaning less than one-fourth of an inch of rain or snow and reddish purple signifying more than one-fourth of an inch. Below that is the humidity monitor; the darker the green, the more humid it is. Finally, wind speed is indicated on the lowest floor, going from pink to magenta when the wind is more than ten miles per hour.

Of course, these new lights can do a lot more than reveal the weather. The designers, Chris Popowich and Cindy Lamauro, have programmed the lights for holiday celebrations and even black-and-gold patterns for our professional sports teams. It is a little more complicated than the days when a man in the lobby flipped a switch after checking the newspaper, but it's a lot more fun—and a lot more energy-efficient.

One other piece of trivia regards the Gulf Tower itself, which was the headquarters of the Gulf Oil Company until 1985. The building stands on the site of the first oil refinery in the United States. Samuel Kier built the refinery in 1853 to refine crude oil, taken from salt wells in nearby Tarentum, into lamp oil. Kier has been called the "Grandfather of the American Oil Industry."

24

INCLINES

"TOURS" DE FORCE

*A*round the world, the vehicles that use tracks to haul people, cars or other objects straight up the side of a hill or mountain are known as funiculars. In Pittsburgh, they are simply called inclines, short for inclined planes. The city is home to two of them, the Duquesne and the Monongahela. They are not the longest or steepest in the world; they are even far from being the longest in Pittsburgh's history. But they are undoubtedly among the most famous on the planet, and they are the only survivors of the nearly two dozen inclined planes that once dotted Pittsburgh's hills.

The operation of a funicular is relatively simple. Two cars, running on parallel tracks, are attached to each other by a cable that is strung through a pulley at the top of the incline. An electric motor turns the pulley and hauls one car up. The other car, as it descends, counterbalances the first car and reduces the amount of energy required to pull the ascending car. The first known funicular was built in Salzburg, Austria, in the seventeenth century to service Hohensalzburg Castle.

The first inclines built in Pittsburgh, in the 1830s, were used to haul coal from the mines that dotted the south slopes of the city. Two of these coal haulers, the Kirk Lewis Coal Incline and the Clinton Iron Works Coal Incline, were situated near where the Duquesne and Monongahela Inclines, respectively, would later be built. Employing inclines on the hilly slopes of Pittsburgh's North and South Sides became a game-changer for the city. Before the coming of the automobile and the electric streetcar, inclines facilitated the movement of goods and people and allowed the city

The Duquesne Incline climbs Mount Washington on a dreary autumn evening. *Photo by Jeffrey Forse.*

to expand. Before inclines began springing up along the south shore of the Monongahela River, for example, Mount Washington and Duquesne Heights were sparsely populated. Most of the residents were German immigrants working the mines of what was then called Coal Hill. The immigrants, who were familiar with funiculars from their native country, became the driving force for the construction of passenger inclines, which they called "seilbahns"—cable cars.

"When the inclines were built, residents now had a choice: ride the incline or walk up 1,400 steps to Mount Washington," said Tom Reinheimer, director of marketing and special programs for the Duquesne Incline. "It wasn't that hard of a choice, especially after working 10 or 12 hours in a hot mill."

In 1870, the Monongahela became the first incline to carry passenger traffic. A year later, the South Twelfth Street Inclined Plane—informally called the Mount Oliver Incline—was built. The Duquesne Incline opened for business in 1877, and as the turn of the century approached, there were seventeen inclines operating around the city. Three of them, the Troy Hill, Fort Pitt and Nunnery Hill Inclines, ceased operation before 1900, and the Ridgewood Incline, in the Perry Hilltop area, burned down in 1900. The rest operated into the 1950s. The most well known of them are the following:

KNOXVILLE

Opened in August 1890, the Knoxville Incline ran from the top of Arlington Avenue, near the intersection with Warrington Avenue, to Eleventh Street on the South Side. The Knoxville was unusual in that its track had a curve about halfway up the slope. Curves on inclines are rare; in Pittsburgh, only the Nunnery Hill Incline also featured a curve. The Knoxville Incline closed in December 1960.

MOUNT OLIVER

Along with the Knoxville, the Mount Oliver Incline was responsible for the development of the Allentown area of the city, which Knoxville and Mount Oliver bordered. It operated from 1872 to 1951, running from Warrington Avenue, near St. Thomas Street, to Twelfth Street on the South Side.

PENN INCLINE

This incline, originally designed to haul coal to the Hill District, ran from Seventeenth Street in the Strip District to Arcena Street on the Hill. Built in 1884, the incline eventually became a passenger and freight incline, used particularly by merchants transporting produce and other goods from the Strip. By the late 1940s, the incline had lost much of its ridership and was open only for a few hours in the morning and afternoon. The Pittsburgh Railways Company petitioned the Public Utilities Commission to allow it to close the incline, and in 1953, its wish was granted.

CASTLE SHANNON

There were actually two Castle Shannon inclines, running side by side, from Mount Washington's Bailey Avenue to East Carson Street on the South Side. Although the inclines were seven miles from the actual community of Castle Shannon, the original Castle Shannon Incline, built in 1825, was part of a railroad that carried coal. In 1861, when the coal mine it serviced was played out, the Pittsburgh and Castle Shannon Railroad extended the railroad down the south side of the mine into the Saw Mill Run Valley to reach other coal mines. In 1874, the company began a passenger rail service to Overbrook and Castle Shannon. In 1891, a new incline with new and more powerful machinery was opened on Mount Washington. A year later, a second incline was built alongside the first, but at a less steep angle. The cars built for the inclines were large enough to carry both people and vehicles. By 1909, the second incline became unnecessary, but Castle Shannon No. 1 continued to be used until 1964.

BUT IT IS THE Duquesne and Monongahela inclines that continue to captivate tourists and ferry Mount Washington and Duquesne Heights residents today. Operationally, the two inclines are almost identical. Both are owned by the Port Authority of Pittsburgh. Their propulsion systems are similar. The Monongahela Incline can carry twenty-three passengers; the Duquesne, twenty-five. About the only physical difference is that the cars on the Duquesne Incline have one large seating area, while those on the Monongahela Incline are divided into three terraced compartments. But in terms of history, the two could hardly be more different.

The Monongahela was the earlier of the two; it is actually the first passenger incline to be constructed in the United States, having opened on May 28, 1870. The site was chosen over what would eventually be the site of the Duquesne Incline because, with its proximity to the Smithfield Street Bridge, it would provide residents better access to the city. The track is 635 feet long and sits at an angle of a little more than thirty-five degrees. Until 1935, a vehicle and freight incline ran alongside the passenger track. Both were owned and operated by the Monongahela Inclined Plane Company until 1964, when the incline was purchased by the port authority.

For all of its history, the Monongahela Incline has been seen as a commuter railway. Yes, tourists do ride it, usually coming from Station Square across the roadway to travel up to Mount Washington to enjoy the view of the city from Grandview Avenue's promenades. But residents heading to and from work downtown have been this incline's economic bread and butter, and in lean times over the past fifty years, it has enjoyed the financial backing of the Port Authority of Pittsburgh.

The Duquesne Incline's timeline has been a bit more colorful. It opened on May 20, 1877, and was owned by the Duquesne Inclined Plane Company until 1964. Its track is 793 feet long, rising at a thirty-degree angle. It seldom could match its sister site in ridership—the Monongahela Incline has a much greater geographic area to draw from, and often people living in the Duquesne Heights section would ride the streetcar or bus over to Shiloh Street to take the Mon Incline for convenience. Over the years, ridership dwindled, and the Duquesne Incline fell into disrepair.

By the early 1960s, the Duquesne Incline's days certainly seemed numbered. In fact, on November 21, 1962, the incline was shut down by the company, which could no longer afford to maintain it. Duquesne Heights residents were outraged, and that same month, a group of people led by David Miller met to discuss how to save the railway from demolition. Miller, an engineer who worked for Jones & Laughlin Steel Corporation out of an office in Gateway Center, was a Duquesne Heights resident who rode the incline to work every day.

The group met with the incline's owners and learned that it would take about $15,000 to bring the railway back to working order. They worked out a deal whereby the company would reopen the incline if the group could raise the necessary funds. Miller and his wife, Ruth, organized people to go door-to-door to solicit donations. Volunteers managed to raise more than $20,000, and on July 1, 1963, the incline reopened.

The following year, the Millers founded a nonprofit organization, the Society for the Preservation of the Duquesne Incline. That same year, the Port Authority of Pittsburgh purchased the incline, as required by a 1959 state law. In 1965, the society reached an agreement with the port authority to operate the incline and has been responsible for turning the incline around financially. The society succeeded by turning it into a working museum and tourist destination. At the incline's lower station, people can actually see the original hoisting mechanism, a drive gear with wooden teeth. The upper level displays a timeline, listing events in the incline's history and notable U.S. and world historical events that have occurred since 1877.

As tour director, Tom Reinheimer is the man who put the Duquesne Incline on the tour map, and he did it in a manner that would make the Millers proud—good, old-fashioned legwork.

"I was seeing ridership dwindling," said Reinheimer, who noted that only about one hundred commuters ride the incline each day. "I looked across the river at the Carnegie Science Center with all the school buses. I went down to the center, but they wouldn't give me their list of school contacts, so I began intercepting random bus drivers as they came into the parking lot. I explained that we offered tours and asked them to spread the word."

Gradually, the message was circulated, and tour companies started including the incline as a potential tour site. Schools began sending students on field trips to the incline, and Reinheimer even created programs for Boy Scouts and Girl Scouts by offering a six-dollar tour that included a Scouting patch for participants.

"We get a tremendous load of kids in here from April to June," he said, "busload after busload, all day long." Indeed, 75 percent of the riders on the Duquesne Incline are tourists—as many as 500,000 per year. Some of them have been rather famous; President Bill Clinton and British prime minister John Major visited the city on February 28, 1994. Major's grandfather, it was discovered, had lived in Pittsburgh for several years in the mid-1800s, working in one of Andrew Carnegie's steel mills.

"As you can imagine, that was quite a day," said Reinheimer, "with the Secret Service all around."

One final piece of incline trivia: Although passenger inclines have been operating in Pittsburgh since 1870—with seventeen running at one point—there has been only one fatal incline accident in the city. That occurred on April 6, 1909, on the St. Clair Incline, when the incline operator passed out. The inclines went out of control; two people were killed and eight others injured in the resulting crash. Another fatality occurred in 1953, when a thirteen-year-old boy was killed on the Knoxville Incline. However, the incline itself was not at fault because, according to police reports, the boy was "hitchhiking" on the back of the incline car and fell off.

Despite this impressive safety record, for a short period of time, one incline was considered to be more dangerous than any other. That was the Duquesne Incline—not because of the incline itself, but because of the risks people had to take reaching and leaving the lower station. As automobiles became more numerous in the city, crossing West Carson Street at the incline became increasingly dangerous. According to a report published by the *Pittsburgh Daily Post*, from January 1923 to May 1926 alone, four pedestrians had been killed and several more injured by vehicles there, making it the second-most-dangerous crossing in the city. In 1932, the city eliminated the "death trap," as the *Pittsburgh Press* called it, by building the covered bridge that people still use today to reach the lower station.

25

IRON CITY

PITTSBURGH'S BEER

There have been quite a number of beers brewed in the Pittsburgh area over the last two centuries. As a matter of fact, in 1899, the Pittsburgh Brewing Company (PBC) was formed as a trust of twenty-one breweries in and around Pittsburgh. But only one brew has become known as the unofficial "official" beer of Pittsburgh: Iron City. Even though the beer is no longer brewed in Pittsburgh—in 2009, brewing was contracted to a brewery in Latrobe, Pennsylvania—Iron City can be found in virtually every bar in the city, and undoubtedly there are old-timers who drink only Iron City. In 2007, when the bankrupt PBC was purchased by a venture capital firm, the name was changed to Iron City Brewing, in recognition of the lager that has stood the test of time in western Pennsylvania.

The history of Pittsburgh beers, and Iron City in particular, is murky, rife with misconceptions and errors. Since the 1980s, Ed Vidunas, a lifelong resident of Pittsburgh's South Side, has tried his best to craft a definitive history of Pittsburgh brewing. His website, pittsburghbrewers.com, contains perhaps the most complete information on the subject. Here is some of what he knows:

Iron City officially became a Pittsburgh beer in 1861, when three gentlemen created the Iron City Brewing Company. Prior to that, any information about Iron City beer or use of the name Iron City is pure conjecture—except this: with the advent of ironmaking in the city, by 1840, Pittsburgh was known in some circles as the Iron City.

Anton Benitz, who came to the United States from Germany in 1838, is generally credited with opening the brewery in 1844 that would eventually become Iron City Brewing Company.

John Miller somehow gained control of the brewery in the 1850s (Benitz reportedly died in 1852) and brought Augustus Hoeveler in as an investor. Edward Frauenheim and Leopold Vilsack also become investors, in 1861.

In 1899, Iron City became one of twenty-one breweries that merged to become the PBC, at one time the third-largest brewery in the country. Even into the 1980s, PBC ranked as high as fifth on the list of largest breweries, before Budweiser began to capture an ever-larger share of the beer market.

Although national beermakers such as Budweiser would blunt PBC's growth, they could never supplant Iron City as Pittsburghers' preferred beer. Even other local breweries such as Duquesne and Fort Pitt failed to steal the title. Says Vidunas: "Iron City always had a good following, and with the sports advertising they had hometown loyalty. Since the 1960s it was just Iron City and Duquesne, but Iron City produced more and became the beer you drank in Pittsburgh."

Perhaps because of its popularity, Iron City was used by the PBC to market a few firsts. In 1962, it became the first canned beer to feature the snap-top can, which Alcoa Company had developed. The following year, it launched the first twist-off cap. Iron City was also the first beer to feature pictures on its cans. Pittsburgh pro sports teams were most often the subjects, with cans commemorating such events as the Steelers' four Super Bowl wins in the 1970s and the Pirates' 1979 World Series win. PBC also is credited with producing one of the first "light" beers, called I.C. Light.

The iconic Iron City Beer logo.
Courtesy of Pittsburgh Brewing Company.

When PBC fell on hard times, so did the beer, as production fell. But Iron City has never lost its status with hard-core city residents, and in 2018, Cliff Forrest, founder of the Rosebud Mining Company in Kittanning, Pennsylvania, bought the company with the idea of bringing the brewery back to prominence.

As for the taste of the beer itself? The company's website describes Iron City as having "notes of sweet corn and smooth, crisp barley malt for a dry finish with very little bitterness." Ed Vidunas says that it gets "a lot of flak from the new craft beer drinkers…but it is clean and not overbearing. You can drink it anytime, and it is best on a hot day."

26

JAZZ

A MUSICAL CROSSROADS

Casual music fans in Pittsburgh may sing the historical praises of radio disc jockeys such as Porky Chedwick, honor the memory of local bands such as Wild Cherry and the Jaggerz that briefly hit the big time or brag about native musical talents such as Christina Aguilera or Wiz Khalifa. But true music lovers understand that if Pittsburgh should be known for anything musically, it is jazz.

When Harlem Renaissance poet Claude McKay referred to the Hill District as "Crossroads to the World," one of the things to which he was referring was jazz. In the first half of the twentieth century, if you were anybody in the jazz world, you spent time in Pittsburgh. You could even say that the phrase made sense geographically: New York was to the east, Chicago and Kansas City were to the west and New Orleans was to the south. All have made their mark on jazz history.

Why Pittsburgh? Like the city's three rivers, a confluence of occurrences fed the growth of jazz here. New Orleans is generally recognized as the birthplace of jazz. A mix of sounds, such as blues and ragtime, played primarily by African American and Creole musicians, was blended to create jazz. The sound made its way north on the riverboats that would ply the Mississippi and Ohio Rivers, and it found itself in Pittsburgh around 1920 in the person of Fate Marable.

Marable, a native of Paducah, Kentucky, made his living playing jazz and dance music onboard steamboats that sailed between New Orleans and St. Paul, Minnesota. According to the book *Jazz on the River*, Marable's family lived in Pittsburgh while Fate played on the riverboats. In the off-season, he would play clubs in Pittsburgh, St. Louis and Paducah, and he found that Pittsburghers loved jazz. More musicians followed Marable, and by the 1930s, jazz was thriving, particularly in the Hill District.

The city became known as a leading developer of jazz talent. Marable is credited with creating the Pittsburgh school of jazz piano. Among its "graduates" were Earl "Fatha" Hines, Erroll Garner, Ahmad Jamal, Dodo Mamaroso and Johnny Costa. "Pittsburgh was a great town for jazz," said jazz guitarist Joe Negri, a Pittsburgh native who got to play with many of the artists who made Pittsburgh their home. "I don't know if you could say we had our own sound, like Chicago or New Orleans or Kansas City. But I think Pittsburgh was on a par with any of those cities."

The book *Jazz in Pennsylvania*, however, does identify a "Pittsburgh" jazz sound. It "combined a strong, straight-ahead urban swing feeling that they merged with a deep blues....The sound was also defined by very strong drumming; drumming that Art Blakey and Kenny Clarke would take to national and international audiences."

The Hill was dotted with dozens of jazz clubs, the most famous of which was the Crawford Grill. Other places where jazz artists developed and/or displayed their talents included the Ellis Hotel, the Webster Grill, the Blue Note, Stanley's and Bamboola. In 1939, Gus Greenlee, the owner of the Crawford Grill, arranged for the great Duke Ellington to meet a young Pittsburgh songwriter, Billy Strayhorn. Ellington was impressed and offered Strayhorn a job with his organization in New York City. Ellington paid for Strayhorn to travel to the Big Apple and gave him instructions to get to Ellington's home in Harlem. The first step after arriving in Manhattan was to go north on the Eighth Avenue subway line, known as the "A" train. "Take the 'A' Train" became the name of the first song Strayhorn composed for Duke Ellington's orchestra.

Like most everything "back in the day," jazz in Pittsburgh was pretty much a men's-only club until Mary Lou Williams came along. Williams, who was born in Atlanta in 1910 but grew up in the East Liberty section of Pittsburgh, was a piano prodigy who began performing in public at the age of seven. Her professional career took her from Pittsburgh to New York and around the Midwest, looping back to Pittsburgh in the 1960s as a teacher of jazz theory. She ended up as an artist-in-residence at Duke University in North Carolina. A composer as well as a musician, she arranged music not only for jazz artists such as Duke Ellington but also for other big band leaders such as Tommy Dorsey and Benny Goodman. A Baptist who converted to

Catholicism, Williams also composed three Masses, the first of which she wrote in 1966 while living in Pittsburgh.

Although musicians of all ethnicities flocked to, and were welcomed in, the Hill District, segregation was still a major piece of the landscape. As a result, white and black musicians belonged to separate unions. However, according to Negri, the black union, the American Federation of Musicians Local 471, "was like a terrific club." The union actually operated the Musicians Club, and after the various bars and clubs closed for the night, black and white artists would head there to continue to jam into the wee hours. *Jazz in Pennsylvania* quotes musician Nelson Harrison as saying, "Whatever you were here for, you found a way to get there rather than go to your hotel room and get some sleep. You didn't want to miss that action."

Pittsburgh produced many fine jazz musicians in the Hill's heyday. In addition to ones already mentioned, local jazz greats include Walt Harper, George Benson, Stanley Turrentine, Billy Eckstine—who, in 1950, outdrew Frank Sinatra when he played the Paramount Theater in New York City—Roger Humphries, Ahmad Jamal, Roy Eldridge, Ray Brown and Nathan Davis, who founded the jazz studies program at the University of Pittsburgh.

The jazz scene in Pittsburgh today is nothing like it was back then; "urban renewal" saw to that. When the city built the Civic Arena, blocks and blocks of the lower Hill District fell to the wrecking ball. Some of those jazz clubs were among the victims. Residents scattered uptown or to other parts of the city, and what was once a thriving, multicultural neighborhood became depressed, poor and mostly black. There is an excellent documentary about jazz in Pittsburgh, "We Knew What We Had: The Greatest Story Never Told," that can be found on YouTube. It is a shame that city officials apparently never knew what they were damaging in the name of progress.

27

KAUFMANN'S CLOCK

THE MEETING PLACE

*E*veryone in the greater Pittsburgh area knows "yinz" words and phrases: "dahntahn" (downtown), "gumband" (rubber band), "redd up a room" (clean), "slippy" (icy), "n'at" (et cetera) and "jeet jet" (have you eaten yet?), to name a few. But if you are a Pittsburgher of a certain era, one before suburban shopping malls, when going into town was almost a necessity if you wanted to shop, watch a movie or see a concert, you also remember a phrase as ubiquitous as "yinz": "Meet me under the Kaufmann's clock."

The brass clock found at the corner of Smithfield Street and Fifth Avenue is perhaps the most well-known landmark in downtown Pittsburgh. Attached since 1913 to the corner of what was once the flagship building of Kaufmann's Department Stores, it was easily found. Several streetcars, particularly those coming from the south hills of the city, traveled down Smithfield Street right past the clock. That, plus the fact that it could be seen from several blocks away, made it a sensible meeting point. In 1998, Mayor Tom Murphy called it "the center of the universe for retailers." The clock has even been the site of lasting memories; some people who have met there have returned to be married on the same spot.

The clock that so many people have met under through the years is not the original Kaufmann's clock, however. The first clock was a four-faced post clock—meaning that it stood atop a metal post—with wood hands. It was installed in 1886, seven years after the Kaufmann building was erected. When the building was renovated and expanded in 1913, the post clock was

The Kaufmann's Clock is undoubtedly the city's most famous meetup spot. *Photo by author.*

removed. However, people complained so much about the loss of the clock that Kaufmann's purchased the 2,500-pound replacement timepiece. This brass clock, designed by the Coldwell Clock Company of New York City, has a face that is braced by two Atlas-like figures that also appear to support an arch over the clock. The arch is topped by a bronze globe. Rumor has it that the clock had been ordered by a bank, which in the end discovered that it couldn't afford the timepiece.

Interestingly, a December 31, 1981 article in the *Pittsburgh Press* states that the clock was built in 1898 and was designed by architect Charles Bickel. The article goes on to say that when the store was expanded in 1913, the northeast corner of the building remained untouched because of the clock. However, this appears to be the only place in which that information can be found. A 1987 article in the same newspaper states that the clock was installed in 1913.

No matter when it was attached to the building, time and the elements took their toll on the clock. It sat silent for years, keeping time, while the soot and grime of the Steel City settled on it. It served as a roosting spot for pigeons and other birds that thanked the clock by leaving their droppings like icing. Finally, in 1987, Kaufmann's executives—as part of a $2.5 million renovation of the historic building—decided it was time to give the clock a facelift.

The work took ten months and cost $30,000. It wasn't an easy task. Workers employed by Architectural Artifacts Inc. to clean the clock's exterior discovered that the dirt coating the bronze was so thick it was seemingly melted on. No chemical cleaner could cut through the muck. In the end, the cleaning crew had to use the type of sand blasters that are typically used to clean bridges. However, sand would have pitted and marred the bronze, so workers improvised by using about one thousand pounds of ground corncobs as the abrasive.

The clock's inner workings were turned over to David McGee, owner of Pittsburgh Clock & Lock Company. Not only did he clean up and repair the inner workings, he also created a pair of wood hands for the clock.

"I was given a picture of the original clock face, with these wooden hands," McGee explained. "They asked me to make replicas of those hands for the refurbished clock. My niece was staying with us while she was attending the Art Institute of Pittsburgh, so we had a drafting table in the house. I used that to make the template and then cut out the hands. We've had to replace one of those hands since, which was easy because now we already had the template."

McGee remembers climbing onto the scaffolding "three or four times" to remount the clock's movements and to help install the hands. "We had to put the new hands on at night, sometime after 11:00 p.m., because they didn't want people to see what the new hands looked like before the clock was unveiled." The refinished clock was revealed at 6:30 p.m. on Monday, November 9, 1987, as part of the city's Light-Up Night.

Since 1987, McGee has been back once, to replace the original movements, which had been designed by Electric Time Inc. of New York City, with computerized movements. "The original movements were friction, and because the corner was windy the hands would sometimes blow off-time. The owner of the May Co. wasn't happy that the clock didn't always tell perfect time. The new system has GPS system set in it."

As well known as Kaufmann's clock is as a meeting place, one anecdote involving the clock is about a meeting that *didn't* take place. In 1983, a feud erupted between Pittsburgh city councilwoman Michelle Madoff and council president Eugene "Jeep" DePasquale. Madoff was promoting a "commuter" tax, which was a voluntary tax on employees who work in the city but live in the suburbs. The tax, Madoff argued, was a way for these people to help pay for city services they enjoy but aren't taxed on. (By law, the city was not permitted to tax non-city residents.) City council passed Madoff's measure eight to one, with DePasquale voicing the only dissent. He thought the idea was ludicrous and told Madoff that if her tax raised more than twenty dollars, he would meet her under the Kaufmann's clock and kiss her "you-know-what."

After Madoff won the bet—various published reports had her collecting anywhere from several hundred dollars to as much as $2,000 from suburban residents—she invited the council president to meet her at 10:00 a.m. on January 24 to pay up. DePasquale never showed, telling the *Pittsburgh Press* later that "I decided…that it may be a little undignified."

28

STEEL MILLS

GOOD, BAD AND UGLY

Pittsburgh's history likely would be far different had it not been for the steel industry. Steel production drove the growth of the city, in terms of both its economy and its population. Steel mills also contributed greatly to the city's major health problems of the late nineteenth and early twentieth centuries, through air and water pollution. But there is no doubt that Pittsburgh would be far less important were it not for its role in helping to build this country.

When cities such as New York and Chicago wanted iconic structures in the late 1800s, they counted on Pittsburgh to supply the materials—especially steel. Pittsburghers made the steel that helped build the Brooklyn Bridge, the George Washington Bridge, the Chrysler Building and the Empire State Building in New York City. When Chicago wanted an awe-inspiring sight for its 1893 World's Fair, it turned to Pittsburgher George Ferris. Ferris designed the world's first Ferris wheel for the fair, and the cages and even the seventy-ton axle for the wheel were made in Pittsburgh and shipped by rail to Chicago.

Andrew Carnegie is generally credited with building the steel industry in Pittsburgh. An investor and owner in foundries and ironworks, Carnegie discovered there was a way to make an even more valuable product when he visited the steel plants of Sir Henry Bessemer in England. Bessemer had developed a process that could make steel more cheaply. Prior to the mid-nineteenth century, steel had limited uses because it was so expensive to make. Iron was used for large products, while steel was used to make cutlery and small tools.

Carnegie took Bessemer's process and made it work on a much larger scale. Soon, Pittsburgh was known as the Birmingham (England) of the United States. (Interestingly, when Birmingham, Alabama, became a major industrial center, it was known as the "Pittsburgh of the South.") America became the world leader in steel production, making sixty million tons a year by 1920. Of the country's total output, Pittsburgh and the surrounding area accounted for 34 percent of the Bessemer steel, 44 percent of the open-hearth steel, 53 percent of the crucible steel, 24 percent of the steel rails and 59 percent of the structural steel.

As Pittsburgh's steel production grew, so did the city. In the last three decades of the nineteenth century, the population increased from about 85,000 to more than 500,000. Many of the new residents were immigrants, and so it could be argued that the steel mills contributed greatly to the rich ethnic heritage of Pittsburgh.

Steel mills are huge operations. They may have coke ovens, blast furnaces, open hearth furnaces, converters, foundries, rolling mills, overhead cranes, casting machines, ladle cars and, of course, the equipment needed to move

Steel mills were Pittsburgh's biggest economic asset—and its worst health problem. *Library of Congress.*

the finished product to trains or ships for transport. Often, mills would operate on both sides of the river, because they required so much land. Jones & Laughlin's plant on the South Side, and the Homestead Works farther upriver, were two excellent examples.

Running a steel mill required tons of energy, in the form of coal, which was cheap and easily accessible in western Pennsylvania. But it was also a very dirty fuel. Burning coal belched clouds of thick, dark smoke that hung over Pittsburgh and coated everything it settled on with ash and soot. Men wearing white shirts could walk out of their offices to go to lunch, and by the time they returned, their shirts would look gray or brown.

Steel mills weren't the only manufacturing plants in Pittsburgh burning coal. But they were easily the largest contributors to the air pollution that plagued the city. As the number of mills increased in the area, so did the level of pollution. On days without a wind to help disperse the smoke, at the height of the day, Pittsburgh would be cloaked in darkness.

In addition to mills polluting the air, they also fouled Pittsburgh's three rivers, discharging waste directly into the water. When combined with refuse from all the riverboats plying the waters to deliver raw materials and haul away finished products, the Allegheny, Monongahela and Ohio Rivers became little more than cesspools. Between 1872 and 1908, Pittsburgh had the highest mortality rate from typhoid in the country.

Residents, or at least business owners, didn't seem to mind all that much. Even though city officials enacted smoke control ordinances, they were not widely enforced. And, in truth, there was very little that could be done technologically at the time to abate the situation. The problem wasn't successfully fought until the middle of the twentieth century, and it actually took a number of different forces: Mayor David Lawrence's strong efforts to enforce strict air pollution controls, the growing availability of cleaner forms of energy and the slow demise of the steel industry in the city.

The beginning of the end for Pittsburgh steel occurred in 1959, when a nationwide strike of steelworkers closed mills for 116 days. During that time, American companies were forced to import steel from other countries, and they discovered that they could buy steel more cheaply this way. The U.S. steel industry never recovered. In the next four decades, twenty-nine U.S. steel firms went out of business. In the twenty-five years after the strike, Pittsburgh's steel production declined by 75 percent, and the city began the shift from a manufacturing economy to a service economy.

Not much is left of the Pittsburgh area's steel mills. The Homestead Works, site of the infamous strike of 1892, is now the Waterfront shopping

The Carrie Furnace in Rankin, a testament to Pittsburgh's once-powerful steel industry, is being preserved and maintained by Rivers of Steel as a history lesson for all. *Photo by author*.

complex. The Jones & Laughlin steel complex, which sat on both sides of the Monongahela just east of downtown, also is gone. In its place are the South Side Works shopping area (south bank of the river) and Pittsburgh's Technology Corridor (north bank). However, the Hot Metal Bridge, which spanned the river and connected the two halves of the mill, still stands. (Amazing fact: During World War II, 15 percent of the steel made in the United States for the war effort crossed the Hot Metal Bridge.)

There are other monuments to the steel industry in the Pittsburgh area, and the Rivers of Steel Heritage Corporation is working hard to make sure they remain. In 1996, the Rivers of Steel Heritage Area was created by Congress. It covers more than five thousand square miles in southwestern Pennsylvania. The organization that oversees this area is, according to its website, "committed to preserving, interpreting, and managing the historic, cultural, and natural resources related to Big Steel and its related industries."

"There is a tremendous amount of history here," said Ron Baraff, director of historic resources and facilities for Rivers of Steel. "It would be a shame to lose it."

Baraff is a native of the Pacific Northwest who moved to Pittsburgh in 2006 and now knows more about the city—especially the steel industry—than most lifelong Pittsburghers. When he talks about the steel industry, as he does during walking tours of the Carrie Furnace in Rankin, across the river from Homestead, his passion for the city is palpable.

Rivers of Steel offers tours, on foot and by boat, to old steel sites along the rivers. Its "Routes to Roots" maps offer people the opportunity to drive to historic sites in the eight counties that surround Pittsburgh. But the organization's primary mission these days is to convince Congress to pass legislation that would create Homestead Works National Park. The park would encompass thirty-eight acres on both sides of the Monongahela River at Homestead and include the Carrie Furnace and the Pump House, the site of some of the bloodiest fighting during the 1892 Homestead Steel Strike.

29

THE PRIMANTI SANDWICH

A UNIQUE MEAL

With all due respect to entrepreneurship, it is almost a shame that you can buy the famous Primanti Brothers sandwich at forty-four locations in seven states. This nearly complete meal between two slices of Italian bread is such an intrinsic piece of Pittsburgh culture—so "Yinzer," if you will—that one could argue that it belongs here and nowhere else.

That is, until you think of all the "ex-Pitts" around the country. Then you realize that Primanti's is just bringing a bit of home out to them.

Wherever you buy it, however, there is no doubting the uniqueness of this combination of ingredients that would make the Earl of Sandwich salivate. You have your choice of meat and cheese, layered with French fries, coleslaw and tomato and spritzed with Italian dressing. The sandwich is as much as six inches tall, once you add the two slabs of bread. (They'll even add onions, if you ask.)

The sandwich, and the diner associated with it, have become so renowned that in 2007, Primanti's was designated an "American Classic" restaurant. The sandwich has gotten airtime on the Food Network, National Geographic and even the Comedy Channel—the last being a mention by Jon Stewart of *The Daily Show* to then-senator Barack Obama, who was planning a trip to the Steel City.

The fame would likely have astounded the Primantis, a trio of Italians from Wilmerding, Pennsylvania, who started selling sandwiches to truckers delivering meat, fish and produce to the city's Strip District. Joe Primanti

The original Primanti Brothers' restaurant in the Strip District. *Photo by author.*

began the venture in 1933 working out of a wheeled cart. Business was brisk—most truckers were arriving in the middle of the night, hungry and with few dining options—and Joe recruited brothers Stanley and Dick to join him.

Soon it became obvious that a cart was never going to keep up with customer demand, so the brothers acquired a storefront on Eighteenth Street between Smallman Street and Penn Avenue. The long, narrow space was open from 3:00 a.m. to 3:00 p.m., five days a week, and was designed to cater to the delivery drivers.

The coleslaw kind of made sense, serving as a substitute for lettuce while giving the sandwich a little extra zest. The fries, however, were an inspiration on the part of John DePriter, the cook and the Primanti brothers' nephew. In 1972, *Pittsburgh Press* columnist Roy McHugh interviewed DePriter, who told him: "A fella drove in with a load of potatoes in the wintertime, and he brought a few of 'em over, to see if they was frozen. I fried those potatoes on our grill and they looked pretty good. A couple of customers asked for them, so what I did, I put the potatoes in their sandwiches."

The rest, as the saying goes, is history.

The list of sandwiches goes more than twenty deep, with available meats including Italian meats, pastrami, turkey, roast beef, ham, steak, fried jumbo baloney and kielbasa. (Herbivores can order the cheese combo, with three types of cheeses in place of meat.) In addition, there are six special sandwiches, such as the Joe, Dick and Stanley: capicola, turkey, roast beef and provolone cheese; and the Carnegie: pastrami, corned beef, Swiss cheese and Primanti Brothers' own Spicy Beer Mustard. The menu lists the number-two seller as the Pitts-Burger and Cheese. There is no best-seller highlighted, but that honor reportedly goes to Iron City Beer.

A lot has changed over the years. The hours at the Strip District diner were gradually lengthened, to the point where it is now open twenty-four hours a day. The Primantis sold the restaurant in 1975 to Jim Patrinos, who added a dining room to the Strip District space and turned the concept into a chain with locations in Ohio, West Virginia, Maryland, Florida, Indiana and Michigan. The clientele has become much more diverse, attracting everyone from tourists to city officials to the occasional celebrity. The menu has become more varied as well, with some locations also offering items such as wings, nachos, flatbreads, pizza, salad and even desserts. And you can order fries on the side. Three types are on the menu: regular; cheese; and Smallman Street, which are fries topped with chili, cheese, bacon, sour cream and jalapeños.

But the makeup of that iconic sandwich will never change.

30

THE TERRIBLE TOWEL

A PITTSBURGH ORIGINAL

*I*f Pittsburghers were to designate one person, place or thing to be "the icon" for the city, you could make an almost unassailable argument for that terrycloth square known as the Terrible Towel. People who have never been to Pittsburgh have not experienced the Duquesne or Monongahela Inclines. They haven't stood at the base of the UPMC Tower and gaped in awe at that unburnished steel skyscraper. They haven't walked to the edge of Point State Park and seen the confluence of the Allegheny and Monongahela Rivers giving birth to the Ohio. But anyone who is a fan of professional football, even if they can't find Pittsburgh on a map, has seen the Terrible Towel at one time or another.

For portions of five decades, the Terrible Towel has been the symbol of Steeler Nation and has been waved in every National Football League stadium in the country. More than that, it has become a symbol for the city around the world. The Terrible Towel has been waved or displayed virtually anywhere Pittsburghers or Steelers fans have gone—even at the summit of Mount Everest. There is even the chance that the towel has been seen by those in the afterlife. After all, one was buried with Pittsburgh mayor Bob O'Connor in 2006.

Often imitated, it still reigns supreme in the sports world while many wannabe gimmicks have been tried and found lacking. The Minnesota Twins have their Homer Hanky. The Atlanta Braves can break out the foam tomahawks to perform the Tomahawk Chop against opponents. And when the Detroit Red Wings hockey team makes the playoffs, you can always expect fans to shower the ice with real octopi. But none of those "traditions" has the universal recognition of the Towel.

The Terrible Towel was introduced in December 1975 before a home playoff game against the Houston Oilers. It is only fitting that the towel's conception is credited to Myron Cope, the flamboyant, nasal-voiced color man for Steelers broadcasts from 1970 to 2005—he is perhaps the quirkiest sportscaster in Pittsburgh's history. But in truth, the towel was suggested to Cope as a gimmick by a sales guy at WTAE, the TV station that aired Steelers games and whose executives felt they needed some sort of symbol to fire up football fans. But Cope quickly embraced the idea, came up with the name and introduced it on a newscast a week before the playoff game. He suggested that fans attending the game bring either a gold or black towel with them to wave.

This was not the first gimmick Pittsburgh sports fans had seen. In 1966, Pirates baseball announcer Bob Prince—an iconic sportscaster in his own right—created the Green Weenie. The symbol was a rattle shaped like a green hot dog, and fans could shake it at the opposition as a hex, or at the Pirates like a good luck charm. Prince himself would exhort fans to shake them at critical points of certain games. That year, the Pirates finished 92-70, but the Green Weenie wasn't enough to carry them to the National League pennant; they finished three games behind the Los Angeles Dodgers. It returned for the 1967 season but quickly died out.

But by the 1970s, Pittsburgh had become a rather rabid football town. So, when fans showed up at Three Rivers Stadium on December 27, 1975, for

Sports fandom's most recognizable symbol, the Terrible Towel. *Wikimedia Commons*.

the first round of the NFL playoffs, an estimated 60 percent of them were carrying gold or black towels. The Steelers won, 28–10, on the way to their second Super Bowl, and the Terrible Towel followed them every step of the way. It would never die.

Cope himself was very much like the Terrible Towel, a colorful original. But when he became the Steelers color commentator, there were more than a few people who thought he—like the symbol he spawned—was a gimmick. According to Mike Silverstein, a journalist and Pittsburgh native who wrote a passionate article about Cope for the 2011 edition of *Behind the Steel Curtain*, one critic compared Cope's voice to "a tornado ripping through a junkyard." Even Cope, when asked to consider taking the job, was skeptical, saying, "Don't kid me. I've heard my voice on tape."

But by the time of his death in 2008, people viewed Cope in an entirely different light. Steelers chairman Art Rooney II said that "history will remember him as one of the great sportscasters of any era." Luke Ravenstahl, Pittsburgh's mayor at the time, recalled Cope as "the heartbeat of the Pittsburgh Steelers in many ways."

So, who owns the rights to the Terrible Towel? If you believe it's the Steelers, you are wrong. Think WTAE, and you'd still be wrong. It was Myron Cope who had the name and the towel trademarked. He held—but never benefited from—the trademarks until 1996, when he donated them to the Allegheny Valley School in Coraopolis. (The Copes' autistic son, Danny, has lived at the school since he was fifteen.) Since then, sales from the Terrible Towel and all the ancillary products, such as ties and even earrings, have generated several million dollars for the school.

But does the Towel have, as some have suggested, magical powers? Well, of course not. That would be silly. Then again, there is this story recounted by Mike Silverstein:

> *On Dec. 21, 2008, the Tennessee Titans defeated the Steelers at Heinz Field, and LenDale White and Keith Bullock stomped on the Towel in its own house. The Titans, who were among the favorites for Super Bowl 43, then inexplicably lost their next eight games. The Steelers, of course, went on to win the Super Bowl. By the end of October 2009, the Titans and their defeated fans sued for peace. A Nashville sportscaster arranged for White and Bullock to sign a towel and ship it overnight to the Allegheny Valley School. Two days later, the Titans defeated the Jacksonville Jaguars, 30–13, for their first win of the season. That, dear friends, is what we call a teachable moment.*

BIBLIOGRAPHY

Alberts, Robert C. *Pitt: The Story of the University of Pittsburgh, 1787–1987*. Pittsburgh, PA: University of Pittsburgh Press, 1986.

———. *The Shaping of the Point: Pittsburgh's Renaissance Park*. Pittsburgh, PA: University of Pittsburgh Press, 1980.

Barnouw, Erik. *A History of Broadcasting in the United States*. Vol. 1. *A Tower of Babel*. New York: Oxford University Press, 1966.

Bockris, Victor. *The Life and Death of Andy Warhol*. New York City: Bantam Books, 1989.

Boucher, John Newton. *A Century and a Half of Pittsburg and Her People*. St. Louis, MO: Lewis Publishing, 1908.

Brownlee, Kevin. "How 500 Years of Weird Condiment History Designed the Heinz Ketchup Bottle." *Fast Company*, December 21, 2013.

Bruhns, Maxine. *The Nationality Rooms*. 4th ed. Pittsburgh, PA: University of Pittsburgh Press, 2000.

Butko, Brian. *Kennywood: Behind the Screams*. Pittsburgh, PA: Senator John Heinz History Center, 2016.

Carnegie, Andrew. *The Autobiography of Andrew Carnegie*. Boston: Houghton Mifflin, 1920.

Conti, John. "Art Deco Style Survives in Pittsburgh—If You Look Around." *Pittsburgh Tribune-Review*, May 4, 2013.

Douglas, George H. *The Early Days of Radio Broadcasting*. Jefferson, NC: McFarland & Company, 2001.

Dunlap, Orrin E., Jr. *Radio's 100 Men of Science: Biographical Narratives of Pathfinders in Electronics and Television*. New York: Harper & Brothers, 1944.

"Duquesne Incline: 'Modern Hill Climbing.'" *Scientific American*, September 18, 1880.

"George Westinghouse: His Life and His Achievements." *Encyclopedia Americana*, 1946.

Jonnes, Jill. *Empires of Light: Edison, Tesla, Westinghouse and the Race to Electrify the World*. New York: Random House, 2003.

Killkelly, Sarah Hutchins. *The History of Pittsburgh: Its Rise and Progress*. Pittsburgh, PA: B.C. & Gordon Montgomery, 1906.

King, Maxwell. *The Good Neighbor: The Life and Work of Fred Rogers*. New York: Abrams Press, 2018.

Lorant, Stefan. *Pittsburgh: The Story of an American City*. Pittsburgh, PA: Esselmont Books, 1999.

Martin, Lawrence. *Mario*. Toronto: Lester Publishing, 1993.

McCullough, J. Brady. "The Evolution of Mario Lemieux: 30 Years in Pittsburgh." *Pittsburgh Post-Gazette*, November 2014.

Nasaw, David. *Andrew Carnegie*. New York: Penguin Press, 2006.

O'Brien, Jim, and Sarah O'Brien Zirwas. *The Chief: Art Rooney and His Pittsburgh Steelers*. Pittsburgh, PA: James P. O'Brien, 2001.

Patterson, Maggie Jones, Michael P. Weber and Rob Ruck. *Rooney: A Sporting Life*. Lincoln: University of Nebraska Press, 2010.

Reynolds, Francis J., ed. "Heinz, Henry John." *Collier's New Encyclopedia*. New York: P.F. Collier & Son, 1921.

Starzl, Thomas E. *Puzzle People: The Memoirs of a Transplant Surgeon*. Pittsburgh, PA: University of Pittsburgh Press, 1992.

Stotz, Charles Morse. *Outposts of the War for Empire: The French and English in Western Pennsylvania: Their Armies, Their Forts, Their People*. Pittsburgh, PA: University of Pittsburgh Press, 2005

Toker, Franklin. *Pittsburgh: A New Portrait*. Pittsburgh, PA: University of Pittsburgh Press, 2009.

———. Society of Architectural Historians, Center for American Places. *Buildings of Pittsburgh*. Charlottesville, VA: Society of Architectural Historians, in association with the University of Virginia Press, 2007.

Whitaker, Mark. *Smoketown: The Untold Story of the Other Great Black Renaissance*. New York: Simon & Schuster, 2019.

ABOUT THE AUTHOR

Paul King is a native of Pittsburgh, raised on Mount Washington with a grand view of the three rivers, Point State Park, the North Side and the downtown skyline. A graduate of Duquesne University, he has been a journalist for more than forty years. He currently lives in Winooski, Vermont, with his wife, Karen, but Pittsburgh will always be "home."

Visit us at
www.historypress.com
....